# Successful Fundraising for Arts and Cultural Organizations

by Carolyn L. Stolper & Karen Brooks Hopkins

 ORYX PRESS
1989

The rare Arabian Oryx is believed to have inspired the myth of the unicorn. This desert antelope became virtually extinct in the early 1960s. At that time several groups of international conservationists arranged to have 9 animals sent to the Phoenix Zoo to be the nucleus of a captive breeding herd. Today the Oryx population is nearly 800, and over 400 have been returned to reserves in the Middle East.

Copyright © 1989 by Carolyn L. Stolper and Karen Brooks Hopkins
Published by The Oryx Press
2214 North Central at Encanto
Phoenix, Arizona 85004-1483

Published simultaneously in Canada

Printed and Bound in the United States of America

∞ The paper used in this publication meets the minimum requirements of American National Standard for Information Science—Permanence of Paper for Printed Library Materials, ANSI Z39.48, 1984.

**Library of Congress Cataloging-in-Publication Data**

Stolper, Carolyn.
  Successful fundraising for arts and cultural organizations / by Carolyn Stolper and Karen Brooks Hopkins.
    p. cm.
  Bibliography: p.
  Includes index.
  ISBN 0-89774-539-6
    1. Arts fund raising—United States—Handbooks, manuals, etc.
  2. Arts publicity—United States—Handbooks, manuals, etc.
  I. Hopkins, Karen Brooks.  II. Title.
  NX765.S78   1989                                           88-38482
  700′.68′1—dc19

# Contents

# List of Charts

# Preface

The purpose of this book is to present the fundraising process as a series of practical steps detailing the mechanics of the successful annual fundraising campaign. We also discuss the roles of the senior staff, volunteers, and board of trustees in fundraising and present in an in-depth way the major funding source categories: businesses, foundations, individuals, and government agencies. Charts appear where pertinent, and all sources referred to in the text are listed in the appendices, along with appropriate service organizations and an annotated bibliography.

The appendices also include examples of such written materials as proposals, invitations, and annual reports. Taken from the institutions for which we work, they illustrate this book's approach to fundraising.

Successful fundraising, however, demands more than an awareness of techniques. The talented fundraiser will rely on his or her judgment and adapt the tools presented here to each specific situation.

# Acknowledgments

We have both had the good fortune of working for cultural organizations with leaders who have given us the opportunity to develop our skills as managers and fundraisers. We would like to express our deep gratitude to Harvey Lichtenstein, Neil Chrisman, and Asher Edelman of The Brooklyn Academy of Music, and to Stephen H. Rhinesmith, Robert Applewhite, and Don Mohanlal of AFS Intercultural Programs, Inc. We also wish to acknowledge the many corporations, foundations, individuals, and government agencies that generously contributed to these organizations and the talented individuals with whom we have worked.

This book could not have been written without the direct assistance of many people. We offer special thanks to Ron Feiner for his legal counsel, to David Bither for his editorial assistance, and to Gaile Burchill for her help in preparing the manuscript.

We would also like to thank Andre Bishop and Anne Wilder of Playwrights Horizons, David Hays and John C. Evans of The National Theatre of the Deaf, and Harry Bagdasian, Ken Bloom, and Bill Kerns of New Playwrights Theatre, as well as Denis Azaro, Martin Berkowitz, Cornelia Bessie, Jacques Brunswick, Mallory Factor, Alan Fishman, Jonathan Gross, Jane Gullong, Rita Hillman, Philip Jessup II, I. Stanley Kreigel, Dr. Stephen Langley, Larry Larson, Eric Marks, Timothy McClimon, Joseph Melillo, Roger Oliver, E. Arthur Prieve, Stephen Reichard, Phil Reynolds, Joel Snyder, Lisa Sommers, Frederic Vogel, John Wessel, the staff of the Foundation Center Library, and the members of the Gotham Club of New York.

Finally, we wish to express our gratitude to our families: Paula and Howard Brooks, Tony and Matthew Hopkins, and Jane and Warren Stolper.

# Introduction

Philanthropy, the giving of one's means to benefit another, is the lifeblood of the hundreds of thousands of nonprofit organizations in America, which in 1983 had assets exceeding $200 billion. The nearly 800,000 nonprofits are dependent upon the support of businesses, foundations, individuals, and the government to survive and function.

American philanthropy is unique. No other nation in the world has as large a number and as great a diversity of not-for-profit organizations, including hospitals, religious organizations, universities, colleges, social service agencies, and cultural organizations. Nearly all Americans believe it is their obligation to support charitable causes. This altruistic philosophy stands in marked contrast to that of most other countries, where philanthropic giving is often exclusively the government's responsibility. The democratic ideal that each person should do his or her fair share, combined with the more contemporary notion of income-tax incentives, has encouraged a wide range of American citizens to become philanthropists. In fact, more than 50 million Americans contribute time and money to the not-for-profit sector.

Our nation's earliest donors were individuals contributing to religious organizations that had established programs to alleviate human suffering. Many of these organizations exist to this day. Due in part to their charitable activities, religious bodies were granted tax exemption. By the beginning of the twentieth century, however, secular organizations had begun to take over many of the charitable functions once performed by religious institutions.

At the same time, individuals, such as Andrew Carnegie and John D. Rockefeller, had amassed great fortunes. These and other wealthy individuals were instrumental in establishing a new vehicle for philanthropic purposes: the general-purpose private foundation. In these early years, health care and education were the primary beneficiaries of contributed funds.

With the outbreak of World War I, Americans for the first time began to make contributions on a massive scale. Four hundred communities throughout the United States established war chests, and the American Red Cross astonished the nation by raising $115 million in one month in 1917. World War I also served as a catalyst for the first substantial giving by American corporations.

The Depression of the 1930s created a new role for government as the primary provider of human services. Private philanthropists turned their attention to seeking remedies for human suffering. Corporate giving to charitable causes was encouraged by the passage of the 1935 Revenue Act, which authorized companies to deduct these contributions from their taxable profits.

In the aftermath of World War II and during the 1950s, both incomes and taxes skyrocketed; the result was a proliferation of family- and company-sponsored foundations established to gain tax advantages. At the same time, Americans first began to contribute substantially to the arts and humanities. In the 1960s, Lyndon Johnson's Great Society initiatives laid the groundwork for widespread cultural support. The establishment of both the National Endowment for the Arts and the National Endowment for the Humanities in 1965, coupled with increased foundation and individual giving, enabled culture in America to flourish.

The sheer number and diversity of today's cultural organizations are a testament to our nation's creative spirit. There are currently thousands of arts and cultural organizations in America, including dance companies, museums and other exhibition spaces, orchestras, zoos, choruses, jazz ensembles, botanical gardens, and theater companies. As the number of cultural organizations has grown, so have their audiences. For example, 97 million Americans have attended museum exhibitions since 1984.

Today, despite the expanded audience, earned income from sales of tickets, merchandise, and services covers only 50 to 60 percent of the operating expenses of a typical cultural organization. Arts and cultural organizations must rely on voluntary contributions for the balance of their income, as do health organizations and educational institutions. The resulting intense competition for the contributed dollar has forced cultural organizations to develop professional fundraising operations in order to survive and prosper.

# Chapter 1
# Institution Building

The word *institution* has been defined as an establishment "founded with authority and intended to be permanent." This definition applies to a cultural organization that is established with a clear artistic or programmatic purpose and with the goal of becoming a permanent part of the community in which it is located. Raising funds is essential to fulfill this purpose and meet this goal. Because fundraising requires a certain level of organizational development, an arts or cultural organization must make a commitment to the process of institution building in order to be successful at raising funds.

Institution building is an organic process whereby organizations evolve from newly formed entities into mature organizations. The use of the word *institution* is not meant to apply only to 100-year-old museums and well-endowed symphony orchestras. All types of arts and cultural organizations, large and small, experimental and traditional, can establish themselves as institutions. The further along the organization is in the institution-building process, the greater its fundraising capability will be.

The process involves defining the purpose and programs of the organization, putting in place and nurturing a board of trustees and a professional staff, and developing a long-range plan. Institution building occurs throughout the life of an organization.

The process begins with a group of individuals dedicated to an artistic or programmatic vision; these individuals form the nucleus of a board of trustees and make the first contributions to the organization. Gradually, as the vision is communicated to more and more people and as it becomes realized in the programs themselves, the organization's audiences will grow, board membership will expand, and the donor base will increase.

There are four broad categories in which funding sources are grouped: individuals, businesses, foundations, and government agencies. A newly formed organization will raise funds more easily from individuals and local arts and humanities agencies, as well as from certain foundations that make grants to begin new projects; as the organization continues the institution-building process, funding from businesses, foundations, and state and federal government agencies will become available. For example, in most cases, before a dance company can be considered for a grant through the dance program of the National Endowment for the Arts, the government agency making grants at the federal level, the company must be in operation for at least three years. Similarly, many businesses and foundations require grantees to evidence a certain minimum budget size, audience size, and level of program activity.

The first step, then, in preparing to raise funds is for management to articulate clearly the artistic or programmatic purpose of the organization. This should be written in the form of a statement of mission. The organization then must work to develop an effective leadership body, which consists of a board of trustees and a professional staff capable of defining the future direction of the organization, developing long-range plans, and delivering what the organization promises.

If the organization is just beginning, it must be incorporated as a not-for-profit, tax-exempt corporation under section 501(c)(3) of the Internal Revenue Code. Only organizations set up in this way can legally apply for and receive grants. It is best to seek an attorney's counsel in filing the necessary documents.

The organization's bylaws are also drawn up at this time. Bylaws are the written rules that set forth the structure for the organization's corporate operations. Bylaws state such information as the official name of the corporation; its purpose; and the powers, duties, and terms of office of the trustees. An organization's bylaws can only be amended by action of the board and must not violate any state laws governing not-for-profit corporations.

## THE STATEMENT OF MISSION

The statement of mission should succinctly define the organization's purpose and programs. The statement should be carefully thought out because it is an important tool in planning, recruiting board members, raising funds, and communicating with the public.

The statement should answer the following questions:

- What are the organization's services and programs?
- For whom are the services and programs intended?
- Which geographic area(s) is (are) served by the organization?

The statement should remain relatively unchanged from year to year; it should be broad enough to allow for organizational growth but not so broad as to allow for wholesale changes in direction. It is essential that the organization's leadership understand the purpose of the organization and be able to articulate its programs. Following are statements of mission written for hypothetical cultural organizations:

The Children's Theatre Company is a professional theater company that produces classical fairy tales, fables, and exceptional contemporary plays for children, parents, and educators in the greater Philadelphia area.

The purpose of the Chamber Music Ensemble is to present to St. Louis audiences a distinctive and varied repertoire of both contemporary and classical music performed by a unique combination of established and emerging artists.

The purpose of Make a Friend International Agency is to provide living and learning experiences for American youth in the Third World.

It is the purpose of the Artists Collective of Washington, D.C., to facilitate the creation of new American drawing, painting, and sculpture by providing studio space to artists and by exhibiting their works in various locations throughout the nation's capital.

The Ballet Company exists to perform a wide range of classical and modern ballets created by the world's finest choreographers, past and present, in the greater Minneapolis–St. Paul area, and to tour these works throughout the upper Midwest.

## EFFECTIVE MANAGEMENT

An effective management—one that provides the leadership and guidance necessary to direct the organization's growth and to achieve its potential—depends on a hard-working and committed board of trustees and a staff of skilled professionals. Management's ability to assess realistically conditions facing the organization is absolutely essential to its operation. This requires a pragmatic and imaginative approach to problem solving in order to maintain the organization's artistic and programmatic standards without overspending. The challenge facing the board and staff is to present programs that not only advance the artistic mission of the organization but also fit within its budget limitations.

## THE LONG-RANGE PLAN

A long-range plan is a written document that defines the organization's future goals and the steps for achieving them. It is integral to institution building. The long-range plan is a blueprint that the board uses to direct and monitor the growth of the organization.

An organization with a plan is one that indeed intends to be permanent. Donors, board members, and the general public feel secure investing their time and money in an organization whose management has a sense of where it is heading. Sharing plans for the future with them can motivate community members and funding agencies to support the organization.

An organization without a long-range plan may be diverted from its original purpose and may be crippled when forced to waste time and money dealing with unanticipated problems. The quality of the programs often suffers immeasurably during crisis periods, and valuable opportunities for institutional growth may be sacrificed. Planning does not preclude risk taking but instead helps in calculating risks and determining those that should be taken and when.

It is the job of the board and staff to formulate this long-range plan. The general guidelines and overall philosophy, however, must be provided by the organization's leaders: the artistic or program director, managing director, and board chair.

The long-range planning process involves a systematic consideration of the current and foreseeable factors influencing the way the organization conducts its business. The process begins with an examination of the strengths and weaknesses of the organization's staff, board, audience or customer size and composition, physical plant, image, reputation, and policies. This enables management to assess the resources available to the organization and to determine those that need to be improved or acquired.

The organization's role in the community must then be analyzed realistically regarding the community's needs, its interest in arts and culture, and its ability to support the organization by participating in its programs and making donations. Demographic and economic trends, as well as the strengths and weaknesses of competing organizations, should be examined. In considering all of these issues, both internal and external, it will become clear that while some factors can be controlled completely by the organization, others can be controlled only partially or not at all. Having taken an inventory of the organization's strengths and weaknesses and having pinpointed where it stands in relation to the community and its competition, management is ready to determine which issues are most critical to the survival and growth of the organization. Long-range goals addressing each of the critical issues should be established.

At this point, examine the statement of mission in light of what has been learned. Does it still hold up? Does it clearly and accurately describe the purpose, programs, audiences, and geographic boundaries of the organization? If not, modifications should be made.

Next, determine objectives and timetables for meeting them that will lead to accomplishing each of the goals. Then, define how the objectives will be met. This means defining tasks, who will undertake them, when they will be undertaken, and what resources will be used. Finally, the organization should design methods for evaluating progress toward achieving the objectives outlined in the plan. Following is an example of an organizational goal and its related objective and tasks.

**Goal**: To develop a more effective board of trustees.

**Objective**: Three potential new board members, each with expertise in one of three areas: fundraising, marketing, and public relations. Candidates will be presented for election to the board of trustees at the annual meeting in December.

**Tasks**:

1. The managing director will solicit names of potential board members from current board members, staff, donors, and colleagues and will draw up a list of these candidates by May 30.
2. The development director will research the list of candidates and determine, with the managing director, five of the most promising by July 30.
3. An informal luncheon will by set up by the development director for each of the five candidates selected. A nominating committee member, the artistic or programmatic director, and the managing director will attend. The luncheons will be held on September 15 and 16, October 1 and 2, and October 15. The budget for each luncheon will be $100.
4. The managing director will arrange a meeting by November 1 with top management and the nominating committee to discuss the candidates. Three candidates will be selected for nomination to the board.

It is quite possible that after objectives and tasks have been determined, it will become apparent that the goal is unreachable or too expensive and should be rejected. This is an important function of the planning process and helps make the plan realistic.

When the planning process has been completed, a long-range plan should be written that consists of the following sections:

- Statement of mission
- Assumptions: internal and external strengths and weaknesses
- Goals
- Objectives and tasks
- Evaluation procedures
- Supplemental information

The supplemental information should include a description of current operations: staff and board responsibilities, facilities, programs, and financial position. Budgets and audited financial statements for the past three years and budget projections for the coming three years should also be included.

Having a long-range plan is no guarantee that an organization will survive and prosper—the plan is only as good as the thinking that went into constructing it and the ability of management to carry it out. If the plan is realistic, it will provide a blueprint for growth and a tool for evaluating the feasibility of new ventures, enabling the organization to face the future confidently.

An organization with creative leadership, a clear statement of mission, and a sound long-range plan is in the best position to deliver consistently quality programs. Such an organization can be relied upon to use funds contributed by outside sources in a responsible and professional way. Funding sources will be more willing to invest in this organization than in one without a fully thought-out purpose and direction.

# Chapter 2
# Leadership

## BOARD OF TRUSTEES

A respected, prominent, and hard-working board of trustees is a very important ingredient in successful fundraising. Persons of high professional caliber with stature in the community are best able to raise the funds needed to ensure the long-term health of an organization. In order to attract such individuals for board membership, it is necessary to define clearly the board's:

- Composition
- Structure
- Recruiting procedure
- Responsibilities
- Fundraising participation

### Composition

To be effective, a board of directors should comprise a balanced mix of individuals who can:

- Contribute funds
- Generate funds from other sources
- Provide professional expertise
- Lend credibility to the organization
- Represent the interests of the community

Very often individuals with these abilities are the wealthy and socially prominent in the community. This is not to suggest that all board members should be wealthy. Ideal board members are persons who can provide social and business connections; who have professional expertise in accounting, advertising, finance, law, management, marketing, or public relations; and who are sympathetic to the aims of the organization. It is also wise to think about community concerns when developing board membership. For example, an orchestra located in a steel-mill town may consider asking a representative of that industry to serve. Be aware of individuals who may use the organization to further their own ambitions. The interests of an individual board member should never override the interests of the organization. Organizations should not overload their boards with staff members. This often occurs when an organization believes it cannot attract qualified individuals to its board or when the staff feels it needs influence on the board. However, professionals and community leaders will not take seriously and will have no interest in joining a board composed of staff members. In addition, conscientious nonstaff board members may object to attempts by staff members to wield power, tire of the internal politics, and resign.

Whether the program director and managing director should serve as board members is a matter of policy to be decided by the board. However, in cases where senior staff do serve it is crucial that they be willing to accept the authority of the board president or chair and to uphold decisions made by the board.

Ultimately, the most effective board is one that is made up of individuals who believe in the mission and goals of the organization and are willing to work to accomplish them.

## Structure

The structure, responsibilities, and procedures of the board—officers, committees, meetings, terms of office—are outlined in the organization's bylaws. The board's structure allows it to conduct the business of the organization in an orderly and efficient manner. A board's officers most often include:

- Chair or president
- Vice-chair or vice-president
- Secretary
- Treasurer

The chair is elected as head of the organization by action of the full board. The responsibilities of the chair are to conduct board meetings according to accepted rules of parliamentary procedure, to appoint board members to committees, and to work closely with senior staff.

The vice-chair should be familiar with the duties of the chair and should be able to assume them in the chair's absence. The secretary's major responsibility is to keep accurate records or minutes of the proceedings of each board meeting. The responsibility for overseeing the financial operations of the organization belongs to the treasurer.

Terms of office ideally should be two or three years, with an annual review to remove those who are not fully participating. A mandatory one-year term usually does not give an individual time to become familiar enough with the organization to be of maximum effectiveness.

Any change in length of term requires action by the full board to amend the bylaws officially.

Board meetings should be scheduled well in advance and should take place at approximately the same time every month, every two months, or every quarter, depending on the needs of the organization. Meetings can take place at the organization's offices or in the business office of a board member. Under normal circumstances meetings should not exceed two hours. Employing strict parliamentary procedure at meetings is a matter of choice, but some type of procedure for voting on issues is needed. Agendas and materials requiring close scrutiny, such as budgets, should be sent to board members at least a week in advance of the scheduled meeting.

As organizations grow in size and sophistication, the in-depth work of the board can be accomplished by committees. Committees, being smaller and more narrowly focused, can concentrate on solving specific problems, freeing the full board of trustees to deal with major policy issues. The following committees are frequently used:

*Executive committee:* This committee is generally made up of the board's officers—chair, vice-chair, secretary, and treasurer—and often the chairs of the standing committees. It formulates institutional policies and consults closely with the senior staff.

*Nominating committee:* This committee works closely with the managing director and other board trustees to recommend and recruit prospective board members. It also assesses each member's participation on the board at the end of his or her term and either recommends re-election or termination.

*Development committee:* This committee works with the development director to formulate fundraising strategies and to supervise campaigns. Whenever possible, the board treasurer should attend meetings of the development committee.

*Finance committee:* This committee oversees the financial-planning process, audit procedures, and the fiscal-management practices of the organization. The board treasurer should serve as chair of this committee.

*Long-range planning committee:* This committee monitors the implementation of long-range plans.

*Ad hoc committee:* This type of committee is set up and disbanded as needed to supervise specific projects, such as review of real-estate issues, investments, fundraising benefits, and other special projects.

## Recruiting Procedure

Recruiting for the board of trustees is an ongoing process that requires careful thought and constant attention. The process begins when that first outstanding individual agrees to serve on the organization's board. Most likely, this board member will want to serve with individuals of similar caliber. If they, in turn, have a positive experience with the organization, both managerially and programmatically, they will recruit other talented individuals for board membership. In this way, as one board member recruits another, it is possible to form a cohesive and effective leadership body.

Board members should be asked regularly for names of colleagues who may be suitable board candidates. These members should also suggest the proper approach to be taken in contacting the prospective trustees.

The senior staff and nominating-committee chair must continually search for individuals who are interested in the organization's programs and who possess the necessary talents for board membership. The organization's donor, participant, membership, and subscriber lists should be researched to determine individuals' business affiliations and special interests. By following social and business activities in the newspapers and by attending community and social events, the senior staff and the members of the board can identify and meet individuals with similar interests in the organization's programs and high profiles in the community.

Once a group of prospective board candidates has been identified, either through research or board recommendation, an effective procedure for recruiting must be established. This procedure includes:

- Familiarizing the candidate with the organization
- Asking the candidate to serve on the board
- Electing the candidate to the board
- Orienting the new board member

The organization could host a reception to which prospective board members are invited. A simple reception may include refreshments followed by a brief performance, demonstration, facility tour, or slide show. This enables the organization's leaders to introduce themselves and the programs to board candidates in a hospitable and festive atmosphere. This cultivation process can also be implemented with individual candidates if the institution prefers not to deal with prospective members *en masse*. The senior staff must have the chance to become acquainted with all candidates and to assess their levels of interest in the organization. However, the candidates should not be asked to serve on the board at this time.

Following the reception, an informal discussion of the candidates should be held by the nominating committee to determine who will be asked to serve. Representatives of the board should then meet with candidates individually to discuss the responsibilities of board membership and how the particular candidate's qualifications may benefit the organization. Candidates should also be encouraged to express their areas of interest and what they would like to accomplish as board members. Once the organization's representatives are ready to recommend candidates to the board, members of the nominating committee and executive committee should be polled for their opinions on each candidate. Following this communication, the nominating committee should convene and draw up a slate of nominees to present to the board for consideration.

The election of candidates should take place at the next meeting of the board of directors. If the nominating committee has done its job, the election will be essentially a formality. The chair of the nominating committee or the chair of the board should nominate the candidates for election to the board of trustees for the term specified in the organization's bylaws. Once the candidates are elected, the board chair should send letters notifying them of their election.

An orientation manual should be prepared and mailed to each new board member with the letter. The manual should be as thorough as possible, containing the following:

- Statement of mission
- History of the organization
- Description of programs
- Bylaws
- Responsibilities of board members
- List of all board offices and committees, describing functions and membership
- Schedule of board meeting dates for the year
- Annual reports for prior two years if available
- Audited fiscal statements for prior two years if available
- Current operating budget
- List of all board members, their affiliations, addresses, and telephone numbers
- List of all staff members and positions
- Brochures, press reviews, and selected press materials

## Responsibilities

The major responsibilities of the board are to maintain the organization's financial solvency and to uphold its programmatic mission. The board carries out these responsibilities by:

- Developing sound management policies and practices
- Participating actively in fundraising
- Recruiting qualified board members
- Hiring qualified senior staff
- Representing the organization in the community

In addition, the board's role with respect to programs is to provide responsible counsel, raise pertinent questions about the organization's financial commitment to its programs, and support programmatic experimentation and creative development through the management plans. Board members should not make day-to-day decisions.

## Fundraising Participation

Board members are the most important participants in the development and execution of annual fundraising campaigns. Board members participate in fundraising by:

- Making personal donations
- Enlisting support from others
- Attending special fundraising events and openings

All board members should contribute to the organization. Personal donations need not be excessive; however, a donation from every trustee is important psychologically to the success of the campaign. Funding agencies are favorably impressed by an organization whose every board member has made a financial contribution to the organization. A board composed of individuals who are both donors to the organization and participants in its activities indicates that it is a well-supported and professionally run organization.

Individual board members should be solicited for their contributions once a year by the board chair. A solicitation by the highest-ranking member of the board is far more effective and appropriate than one initiated by a staff member.

Board members should provide contacts at foundations and in the business sector, as well as among private citizens. The development director should determine whom each board member will solicit for a contribution on behalf of the organization. Once the board member has provided contacts, it is the responsibility of the development director to work with that board member to make the appeal.

Board members are expected to attend premieres, openings, and special fundraising events where donors and prospective donors will be present. The attendance of board members at these events lends considerable credibility to the organization. It is also very helpful to the organization's fundraising efforts if board members establish personal relations with those who support the organization.

## SENIOR STAFF

The senior staff is as important as the board of trustees in determining the future health and growth of the organization. To ensure that the organization grows and prospers, the board of trustees and senior staff must work together, sharing their sense of pride and ownership with donors, audience members, and the community.

The senior staff of the arts or cultural organization usually includes an artistic or program director, a managing director, a development director, a finance or business manager, and a marketing director. As organizations grow and become more sophisticated, other positions are created that may entail responsibilities previously included in the job descriptions of the positions mentioned above or in new areas of responsibility.

The artistic or program director is often hired by the board of trustees. The selection of the development director, although usually made by the top staff director, will be heavily influenced by the board because of the close relationship necessary between the board and development director.

In order to hire qualified individuals, the board must first define the responsibilities of each position as well as the attributes and qualifications required. The board must then take time to search for, interview, and check the references of qualified candidates. The board should communicate a timetable for performance review, such as every six months or once a year, and, if appropriate, a letter of agreement should be signed when an individual is hired.

## Artistic or Program Director

The primary responsibilities of program directors are to establish and carry out the programs of the organization. They must also be willing to participate in fundraising and in the recruitment of board members.

Good program directors must not only be skilled in their field, but must also be able to inspire the board and staff. They should understand the business of creating artistic and cultural programs and have a working knowledge of fundraising, marketing, and financial management so that they can select programs compatible with the mission and financial capability of the organization.

Program directors are typically the most effective spokespersons for the organization. They must be willing to share their vision with colleagues as well as with the staff, board, audience, and community. This is important not only in raising funds and recruiting board members but also in generating goodwill in the community. Board members and representatives of funding agencies often want to become acquainted with the organization by establishing a one-to-one relationship with the person who is directly responsible for its programs. The artistic or program director can reinforce the organization's presence in the community by attending community functions that do not necessarily involve the organization.

## Managing Director

Managing directors direct the administration that will allow the organization to realize its artistic or cultural goals. They must work in partnership with the board of trustees and with the program director, supporting programs while maintaining realistic fiscal and management policies. If the organization has no development director, then the managing director also assumes the duties of development director as discussed below.

Just as program directors must strive to understand the business practices of the organization, managing directors must be knowledgeable about the art form or program thrust and sensitive to the aims of the organization.

## Marketing Director

Marketing directors are responsible for planning and implementing earned income campaigns to sell the organization's products and services. These products or services can include tickets, subscriptions, publications, tours, admissions, programs, courses, or merchandise. To this end, marketing directors oversee promotion and advertising, group sales, press relations, audience development, telemarketing and direct-mail campaigns, and promotional events as they relate to selling the organization's product. They must be energetic, creative, and able to find new ways to focus the attention of key markets on the organization and its products and services.

## Finance Director

Finance directors manage the organization's cash and see that bills are paid and receipts collected. Responsibilities usually include preparing financial reports, cash flow statements, and budgets; submitting all federal, state, and local tax forms; monitoring accounting systems; and administering health, welfare, and pension plans for employees.

Finance directors must understand the principals of accounting and be skilled in money management. They must also be able to work with each department in the organization to set up systems that are flexible enough to meet each department's cash needs in a timely way and that provide an accurate record of the department's business transactions.

## Development Director

Development directors are responsible for planning and implementing annual fundraising campaigns. They must be energetic and capable of sustaining the momentum of the campaign.

Development directors work closely with board members and senior staff to determine viable fundraising goals and to create an ambitious yet realistic fundraising plan that will enable the organization to undertake challenging projects. The fundraising campaign will always have a better chance of succeeding if the programmatic and financial plans are realistic and well coordinated.

## VOLUNTEERS

According to a study by Independent Sector entitled "The Charitable Behavior of Americans," people who volunteer for an organization contribute more funds than those who do not directly participate. Giving and volunteering go hand-in-hand. It is wise for an arts or cultural organization to devise ways to incorporate volunteers into its fundraising strategy. Volunteers not only carry out the actual work of many not-for-profit organizations; they are also instrumental in helping the organization raise funds. They do this by contributing themselves, becoming board members, asking others to contribute, conducting small fundraising events, working at galas or phonathons, and providing expertise and information that can enhance the fundraising campaign.

According to Independent Sector, in 1985 an estimated 43 million Americans volunteered either five or more hours a week or contributed at least 5 percent of their income to the charity of their choice. Forty-eight percent of the adult population, or 82 million people, from all walks of life, volunteer in some way. Volunteering is clearly a national pastime.

As further evidence of this, corporations are rapidly becoming primary motivators for volunteering among their employees. According to Volunteer, The National Center, in 1985, more than 600 corporations sponsored some type of activity to involve employees in volunteer jobs in the community. The 1986 issue of *Giving USA* reported that more than 200 companies have structured programs through which employees can volunteer, and an increasing number of businesses have set up employee volunteer funds that disburse small gifts to not-for-profits in which employees volunteer.

Volunteers can make the difference between a successful campaign and one that never reaches its full potential. In order to incorporate volunteers successfully into fundraising:

- Clearly outline their responsibilities
- Train them to carry out these responsibilities
- Prepare them to solicit funds effectively
- Monitor their progress and reward successful performance

## Outlining Volunteer Responsibilities

Because volunteers do not receive salaries for their work, organizations often do not take the necessary step of clearly outlining for them the responsibilities of particular jobs and what is expected of them. The organization should interview potential volunteers with an eye to the kinds of skills needed for the job at hand in much the same way as candidates for salaried positions are interviewed. Establishing an acceptable work schedule, defining the bounds of the volunteers' responsibilities, and clarifying which decisions must be made by staff and which can be made by volunteers are especially tricky issues that can lead to major problems if not clearly communicated up front. It might be a good idea to draw up volunteer job descriptions or sign an informal letter of agreement. All individuals work better when they know how their performance will be judged; volunteers are no different.

## Training Volunteers

All volunteers, regardless of the particular jobs they will be performing, require a general introduction to the organization and its programs. This could be accomplished by simply putting together a packet of information on the organization, including an annual report and program brochures, and giving them a tour of the facility. Additional training will depend on the jobs they are assigned to do.

In this discussion, the focus will be on training key volunteers to solicit funds in face-to-face meetings. These volunteers could be board members as well. Using volunteers in telefundraising and special events is discussed later, in Chapter 6 and Chapter 8, respectively.

Training volunteers to solicit funds generally involves helping them understand the motivations behind giving, preparing them for a visit, and providing a forum for them to practice before actually having to ask "for real."

Generally, it is thought that tax benefits are the main reason for contribution to charity. Although certainly an important factor in giving, this is rarely a primary motivation.

Individuals give because:

1. They are committed to the mission of the organization and believe in its programs and activities;
2. They are involved directly in the organization, as participants, subscribers, or volunteers;
3. They wish to be recognized publicly for their good deeds and have a certain sense of community responsibility;
4. They are asked by someone they respect.

It is also helpful in setting the stage for volunteer solicitation to shift the emphasis from asking for money (which is a terrifying prospect to many people) to offering an opportunity to make a difference by becoming involved in the fine work of the cultural organization.

## Preparing Volunteer Solicitors

This is a critical step in the process. Because an organization usually gets only one shot at asking an individual for funds, it must be the best effort that organization can muster. If it has been decided that a volunteer or board member is the best person to do the asking, then it is incumbent upon the development director to prepare the volunteer thoroughly. It is recommended that Chapter 3 be read in its entirety before undertaking the task of training a volunteer to solicit. Chapter 3 describes how to implement an annual fundraising campaign.

Preparing the volunteer to solicit involves developing research profiles of the assigned prospects and going over the information with the solicitor. Since the intent here is to minimize surprises, the profiles should present pertinent facts about past involvement with the organization by the prospects and their families as well as their financial situation and general philanthropic activities. See Chapter 3 to learn how to prepare a research profile. The solicitor should also be instructed on the various ways in which the individual may contribute, such as with cash grants, or gifts of stock or real estate. Lastly, the solicitor must be knowledgeable about the history, goals, and current programs of the organization. Conducting some practice rounds with the volunteer is a good idea.

## Monitoring Progress and Rewarding Success

Since volunteers receive no wages for their services to the organization, they should be paid with respect and prompt service. The best volunteer/staff relationships are built on mutual trust and respect. Call key volunteers often to let them know the organization is counting on them; offer to prepare letters, materials, or special visual aids for them. This kind of service not only fosters a positive relationship but also allows the organization to ensure a certain standard of professionalism in the documents and letters used to represent it. Frequent calls also help uncover any real or potential problems that might prevent the volunteer from following through on the solicitations.

When volunteers succeed, they should be duly honored and recognized. Special volunteer events and social get-togethers should be planned as a regular part of the organization's activities. In addition to receiving personal thank you letters from the organization's leaders, successful volunteers can be featured in the organization's newsletter. Many organizations present a special award to the volunteer who contributed the most service to the organization.

# Chapter 3
# The Annual Fundraising Campaign

An annual fundraising campaign is a step-by-step process of raising a specific amount of money over a set period of time. The annual campaign should run for a span of one year, corresponding to the organization's fiscal year, and should begin again at the start of the next fiscal year. This regular annual cycle allows the organization to monitor its relationship with each funding source, track progress toward reaching fundraising goals, and evaluate the success of each year's fundraising efforts in comparison with past campaigns. Conducting a carefully orchestrated fundraising campaign on an annual basis enables an organization gradually to build a base of support from a broad range of donors. It is a far healthier strategy to seek smaller grants from many different sources than to pursue large grants from only a few. An organization takes a great risk by counting on the generosity of a small number of donors.

The annual fundraising campaign approach also helps the organization avoid the damaging situation of having to appeal for emergency financial support. Funding agencies typically do not respond positively to appeals from an organization in a financial crisis. They not only are reluctant to risk funding an organization with serious financial difficulties but also are often unable to make a contribution quickly enough to be of assistance. Furthermore, an organization's credibility in the philanthropic sector diminishes substantially when it appeals for emergency support. It can often take years to rebuild a damaged reputation.

In certain disastrous situations, however, it is appropriate to seek support if the crisis is not the obvious result of mismanagement. For example, an organization that suffers extensive damage as a result of a flood or fire may successfully raise funds to rebuild by making an emergency appeal.

A successful fundraising effort will depend on a well-conceived and well-executed campaign, which requires that the organization:

- Determine goals, strategies, and timetables
- Establish a record-keeping system
- Research renewals and prospects
- Develop cultivation plans
- Solicit funding sources
- Build a sense of ownership

A section on the use of computers in implementing an annual fundraising campaign is included toward the end of this chapter.

## GOALS, STRATEGIES, AND TIMETABLES

The goals of the fundraising campaign can only be determined once the programs for the coming year have been selected. A strong programmatic mix is of great advantage to the development director in raising funds. Therefore, it is essential that the programs and their costs be determined far enough in advance of the new fiscal year, usually six months to a year or more for larger initiatives, to allow adequate time to plan and implement the fundraising campaign.

Determining the programs is a matter of considering tentative projects, projecting income and expenses for each of the projects, and then selecting the programs that have both artistic or cultural merit and financial viability. In most cases, the artistic or program director, in consultation with the managing director and other senior staff members, makes the actual program selections, which are subsequently approved by the board. Once the programs have been approved in concept by the board and senior staff, the development director must devise a fundraising strategy that will meet the financial needs of the programs. A useful device for determining the fundraising potential of a particular project is the fundability index (Chart 3.1).

Materials should be prepared that present the history of the organization, its program and senior personnel, and its tour or exhibition schedules. Press reviews and other documents should be gathered. The development director may also elect to produce special fundraising brochures aimed at a particular funding-source category, such as the business community.

Based on the costs of the programs, the development director determines contributed-income goals; the marketing director, who is responsible for sales fees and admissions, determines earned-income goals. The final program decisions are based on a realistic analysis of the contributed-income and earned-income projections.

The contributed-income projections must take into account the fundraising history of the organization, the economic climate, changes in patterns of donor contributions, the number of past appeals made to a particular donor, and the attractiveness of the programs to specific donors. It should be kept in mind that because fundraising depends heavily on personal contacts developed over time, it can often take two to three years of repeated appeals to a likely prospect before a grant is received.

## CHART 3.1 FUNDABILITY INDEX

---

PROGRAM: _____

PERSON RESPONSIBLE: _____

| Rating Key: | 5 = Excellent | 2 = Needs Work |
|---|---|---|
| | 4 = Good | 1 = Weak |
| | 3 = Fair | 0 = Non-existent |

---

1.  *External Need*                                    Rating: _____
    Does the program meet existing social, economic, educational, and cultural priorities? (Delineate reasons why program is important.)
2.  *Internal Need*                                    Rating: _____
    Is the organization's mission and number of participants or audience numbers enhanced? (How will this be achieved?)
3.  *Uniqueness*                                       Rating: _____
    Is a similar program already in operation by another organization? (How is the program unique? Does it represent an innovative solution to a problem?)
4.  *Endorsement*                                      Rating: _____
    Has the program received educational or cultural endorsements at national, state, and/or local levels in cities where program activity will be taking place? (Are these available to include in proposals?)
5.  *Impact*                                           Rating: _____
    How many people are expected to benefit from the program, and how will they benefit?
6.  *Measurable Results*                               Rating: _____
    Does the program have an evaluation mechanism built into it to measure how the program has met the internal and external needs?
7.  *Fundraising Sources*                              Rating: _____
    Is there a sufficient number of interested prospective donors in the city where program activity will be taking place? Do you know actual names of corporations, foundations, and individuals with an interest in the program?
8.  *Visibility/Public Relations*                      Rating: _____
    Do opportunities exist for providing P.R. and visibility for the organization in the city where program activity will be taking place?

---

The development director determines contributed-income goals by projecting the amount of contributed support from donors that contributed in the last fiscal year in each of the four categories: businesses, foundations, individuals, and government agencies. Gifts from this group should be projected at 90 percent, since there is always the possibility that some gifts will not be renewed or may be renewed at a lower amount.

The development director should then project the number and amount of new gifts in each of the four major contributor categories as part of the total campaign goal. A conservative percentage—generally between 35 and 50 percent—of funds from currently identified prospects should be used.

Currently identified prospects include sources that have been identified and contacted but have not undergone the formal solicitation process, as well as those that have received proposals from the organization and have expressed an interest in making a grant. Also included in this category are sources that have discontinued their support for a period of time and are now likely to give again. Finally, a conservative estimate should be made of proceeds from special events, such as gala benefits, to be undertaken during the year. The campaign goal equals the amount of money already in hand or pledged at the beginning of the fiscal year plus the funds expected from renewals—projected at 90 percent—plus a percentage of currently identified prospects—projected at 35 to 50 percent—plus a conservative estimate of proceeds from special events. Please refer to Chart 3.2, the campaign support plan, for an illustration of this.

The development director also constructs a campaign timetable. This timetable lists the dates when special events will take place and the deadlines for appeals to businesses, foundations, individuals, and government agencies. Since many funding agencies prepare their contribution budgets well in advance of the actual funding year, the organization's requests for funds must be made at the appropriate time in order to be eligible to receive funds budgeted for the following year.

When all projections, goals, and timetables have been established, the development director reviews them with the managing director and the board's development committee. The development committee examines the campaign projections, goals, and timetables in detail. At the next board meeting, the campaign plan and strategy are reviewed and approved. The development director then implements this plan, enlisting the help of board members and staff as needed. Regular meetings with the managing director, development director, and development committee should be held throughout the year to track the campaign's progress.

In addition to meeting fundraising goals, the development director is responsible for running the fundraising campaign efficiently and within certain budget restrictions. As a rule of thumb, no more than $.20 to $.30 should be spent to raise $1.00. There are mitigating circumstances that sometimes require larger expenditures than this general rule, such as large-scale donor acquisition telefundraising campaigns, changeover to new computer systems, or the hiring of a consulting firm for major endowment or special capital campaigns. It is important that funds be raised to support programs, not to support fundraising. On the other hand, the institution must ensure that the fundraising staff have adequate equipment and personnel to meet their goals.

## CHART 3.2 CAMPAIGN SUPPORT PLAN

### Fiscal Year _____

| | TOTAL FUNDS RCV'D (Actual) | TOTAL FUNDS PLG'D (Actual) | TOTAL FUNDS EXPCT'D (Projected at 90%) | TOTAL FUNDS PROJ'D FROM CURRENTLY IDENTIFIED PROSPECTS (Projected at 35%–50%) | CAMPAIGN* GOAL |
|---|---|---|---|---|---|
| **PRIVATE** | | | | | |
| FOUNDATIONS | | | | | |
| BUSINESSES | | | | | |
| INDIVIDUALS • Patrons • Lower Level | | | | | |
| SPECIAL EVENTS | | | | | |
| Sub-Total | | | | | |
| **PUBLIC** | | | | | |
| FEDERAL | | | | | |
| STATE | | | | | |
| MUNICIPAL | | | | | |
| OTHER | | | | | |
| Sub-Total | | | | | |
| **TOTAL** | | | | | |

*The campaign goal equals the total funds received, pledged, and expected, plus the amount projected from currently identified prospects.

## THE RECORD-KEEPING SYSTEM

A comprehensive record-keeping system must be set up to store information pertaining to donors and new prospects and to organize information to track campaign progress. The following discussion outlines the elements in a manual record-keeping system.

It is enormously helpful, however, to use a microcomputer for this job. There is a section toward the end of this chapter on using a computer in fundraising. Computers, because of their sophisticated information-management capabilities, have implications beyond merely helping organize and store donor records. The section will also cover using the computer for research and document preparation, for targeting the best prospective donors, and for helping build a sense of ownership in donors. It will be helpful to read all of this chapter before turning to the computer section.

The success of any record-keeping system depends on recording accurate information as soon as it is known. All of one's hard work in cultivating a prospect or donor can be totally undone if a slip-up occurs as a result of incorrect information. A record-keeping system also provides continuity in conducting the campaign from year to year and facilitates easy transitions when personnel changes occur.

The basic record-keeping system includes a:

- Principal record file
- Permanent correspondence file
- Current campaign tracking file
- Campaign status report
- Contribution processing file

## Principal Record File

The record-keeping system is based on an alphabetical principal record file. Index cards for current and prospective donors are produced and filed separately and subdivided by type of funding source, i.e., business, foundation, individual, or government agency. The cards must be kept up-to-date, neat, and accurate, reflecting changes in addresses, funding-source personnel, and other significant information. It is helpful to design a standard format for the principal records and to print them in quantity (see Chart 3.3). The information listed below should be recorded on the card for each business, foundation, and government agency solicited. The card for an individual is basically the same, except, of course, that it omits information pertaining to institutions.

1. Full name of funding source
2. Address and telephone number
3. Names and titles of the primary contacts at the funding source
4. Salutation
5. Indicate whether donor or prospect and whether business, foundation, government agency, patron, or lower level giver
6. Names of top officials or trustees
7. Special interests, geographic preference, and restrictions
8. Other information, e.g., names of spouse and children, special likes and dislikes
9. Funding history by year
   a. How much money was received and when
   b. For what purpose
   c. To what appeal did donor respond
10. Name of the referee—the individual who makes the appeal on behalf of the organization, i.e., board or staff member

11. Name of the contact—the individual to whom the referee sent the appeal
12. How much was requested
13. When appeal was made
14. Application and final report deadlines

## CHART 3.3 PRINCIPAL RECORD FILE

(Front of Card)

**PRINCIPAL RECORD FILE**

NAME: _____
       (Firm or Individual)

ADDRESS: _____
_____ ( ) _____

| CONTACT NAME | TITLE | PHONE | REFEREE |
|---|---|---|---|
| | | | |
| | | | |
| | | | |
| | | | |

PRIMARY INTERESTS: _____
_____

APPLICATION DEADLINE: _____

(Back of Card)

| CAMPAIGN YEAR | AMOUNT RQST'D | DATE RQST'D | SENT BY | AMOUNT RCV'D | DATE RCV'D | COMMENTS (PURPOSE OR APPEAL) |
|---|---|---|---|---|---|---|
| | | | | | | |
| | | | | | | |
| | | | | | | |
| | | | | | | |
| | | | | | | |
| | | | | | | |
| | | | | | | |
| | | | | | | |
| | | | | | | |

Basic information, such as names, addresses, and special interests, is recorded when the prospect is researched. All other information is recorded as the solicitation progresses.

The principal record file is used as a quick reference and as an ongoing record of the general content and timing of a specific appeal. Each file summarizes all important facts regarding the funding source and its relationship to the arts or cultural organization.

## Permanent Correspondence File

While the principal record file provides a quick reference on each funding source, the permanent correspondence file is an in-depth chronological record of the organization's relationship with a funding source over time. The files should include a folder for each source, containing copies of all proposals, reports, and letters sent from the development office, as well as letters received from the source. The folders should be organized alphabetically within the following sections: businesses, foundations, individual donors, and government agencies. Supplementary information on a funding source, such as pertinent newspaper and magazine clippings, annual reports, contribution history, and other notes, should be kept in this file.

Individual folders for each board member may also be kept in the permanent correspondence file. Each director's folder should contain correspondence, an official biography, contribution history, and lists of funding and community contacts.

## Current Campaign Tracking File

In order to track active campaign appeals, it is helpful to set up a current campaign tracking file. The file should contain copies of all the original proposals and follow-up letters that were sent to major funding sources during the campaign. By regularly perusing this file and by referring to the principal record file, the development director can keep on top of each request. Notes indicating telephone conversations that have taken place can be attached to the appropriate appeal.

Once a grant has been awarded or denied, all correspondence with the particular funding source should be removed from the current campaign folder and placed in the permanent correspondence file.

## Campaign Status Report

The campaign status report is a chart that enables the development director to track the progress of the campaign against the goal. The status report lists alphabetically each funding source contacted in the four contributor categories—businesses, foundations, individuals, and government agencies—and records the amount requested, the amount pledged, and the amount actually received. Funds generated through special events typically appear in two or more donor categories; because these funds are often given in addition to general or project funding contributed by the funding source, it is a good idea to include special events as a separate funding source category. At the end of every month the development director should compile a summary sheet (see Chart 3.4) that indicates by category the totals of gifts received and pledged as compared to the campaign goals. The summary sheets can be used to report the progress made in the campaign to the board of trustees and management.

## CHART 3.4 CAMPAIGN STATUS REPORT SUMMARY

### Month and Year _____

|  | TOTAL FUNDS RCV'D (Actual) | TOTAL FUNDS PLG'D (Actual) | TOTAL FUNDS REC'D & PLG'D | CAMPAIGN GOAL |
|---|---|---|---|---|
| **PRIVATE** |  |  |  |  |
| FOUNDATIONS |  |  |  |  |
| BUSINESSES |  |  |  |  |
| INDIVIDUALS • Patrons • Lower Level |  |  |  |  |
| SPECIAL EVENTS |  |  |  |  |
| Sub-Total |  |  |  |  |
| **PUBLIC** |  |  |  |  |
| FEDERAL |  |  |  |  |
| STATE |  |  |  |  |
| MUNICIPAL |  |  |  |  |
| OTHER |  |  |  |  |
| Sub-Total |  |  |  |  |
| **TOTAL** |  |  |  |  |

## Contribution Processing File

Once a contribution is received, the check should be photocopied and a numbered receipt issued. The original receipt is sent to the donor with a thank you letter. One copy of the receipt is given to the organization's finance office along with the actual check, and another copy is filed in the development department's contribution-processing file. Photocopies of the check and thank you letter are also filed in the permanent correspondence file.

## RESEARCHING RENEWAL CANDIDATES AND NEW PROSPECTS

Researching is an extremely important step in the fundraising process. It allows the development director to identify those businesses, foundations, individuals, and government agencies that are most likely to support the organization. Rather than being wasted on prospects that have no interest in the organization, energies can be directed toward pursuing promising funding sources. Research of renewal candidates and new prospects also helps uncover potential board members and provides a better overall understanding of the workings of the philanthropic sector.

Accurate lists of renewal candidates and new prospects should be assembled in each of the four contributor categories: businesses, foundations, individuals, and government agencies. Each list should include the full name and address of each funding source; if the source is an agency or firm, the name of the contact person and the names of trustees or top officials should also be included.

There are many directories, organizations, and individuals that can be consulted during the research process. A useful device for recording the information gathered is the corporate research profile (see Chart 3.5).

The development director begins by constructing a list of renewal candidates in each contributor category. The list must include all donors from the prior year; these sources must be solicited annually for contributions. Except in the case of a multi-year pledge, there is no way of knowing whether a gift will be renewed unless the donor is asked.

The list of new prospects should include promising sources as well as previous donors that have not contributed recently. It is important to continue soliciting those that have not contributed for several years, because circumstances preventing them from contributing may have changed in the organization's favor. However, if a reason has been given for denying support, and if there is evidence that the reason still holds, then do not make a request.

A likely new prospect is a source that has demonstrated an interest in the organization, such as through a subscription purchase, or through attendance at a single performance or special event. Equally promising are personal friends and business colleagues of board members. Other likely new prospects may be those that support similar organizations in the community or region.

The best way to identify these prospects is regularly to peruse the organization's subscriber, membership, and ticket-buyer list, as well as the programs and annual reports of similar organizations in the area. Short lists of new prospects should be circulated among board members on a regular basis.

## CHART 3.5 CORPORATE RESEARCH PROFILE

**CORPORATE DATA**

XYZ Company
Address
City, State, Zip
Telephone

WHO RUNS THE COMPANY

RECENT BUSINESS ACTIVITY: Year _____

Sales: _____
Profits: _____
Rank: _____
Employees: _____
Major Products/Industry: _____

DOMESTIC OPERATIONS

INTERNATIONAL OPERATIONS

**PHILANTHROPIC DATA**

XYZ Company Foundation
Address
City, State, Zip
Telephone

Contact Name and Title

WHO RUNS THE FOUNDATION

RECENT PHILANTHROPIC ACTIVITY

How Much They Give: _____
Grant Range: _____
Domestic Giving Policy: _____
International Giving Policy: _____
Application Procedures: _____
Sample Grants: _____
Giving History at Organization: _____
On File at Organization: _____


Date Prepared: _____
By Whom: _____

Each prospect should be evaluated in terms of:

- Special interests
- Geographic preference
- Economic condition
- Preferred type of support

Culture is one of many philanthropic causes receiving charitable support. Most businesses, foundations, and individuals contribute to those causes in which they have a special interest. It is a waste of time to pursue prospects that have demonstrated no interest in the organization's particular area of activity unless there are exceptional circumstances, such as close personal contacts at the board level.

Donors often prefer to support organizations that are located within specific geographic areas. Some corporations, for instance, support organizations in communities where they have plants or branch offices. Therefore, it is important to research all funding sources in the same locality as the organization. Only organizations with national impact will be successful in raising funds outside their own regions unless, of course, involved individuals have close personal contacts at funding sources in other regions. Another exception to this rule may be organizations that regularly tour to other locations.

The financial condition of prospective donors also influences their ability to make contributions. During economic downturns, for example, many businesses will cut back giving in all but a few primary areas; in extreme cases, giving may be cut out entirely. When analyzing funding prospects in the business community, it is important to determine the financial condition of each business as well as the economic condition of the industry and related industries.

The type of support a particular donor gives and the usual amount of the contribution should also be determined. Five basic types of financial support are given: general; project; matching or challenge; capital; and endowment. The two latter types, capital and endowment, are not considered part of an annual campaign to raise funds for current operations.

*General support*: This type of funding is unrestricted in its use. General support typically covers operating expenses, such as telephone, salaries, administration, and supplies, and can be requested on an annual basis.

*Project support*: This type of funding is restricted to the specific project for which the institution has requested funds. Often project grants are awarded on a one-time-only basis and are not renewable.

*Capital support:* This type of funding is given for building, renovation, or construction projects, as well as for the purchase of equipment. Capital support is usually given on a one-time-only basis. Grants for construction projects are frequently referred to as bricks-and-mortar grants.

*Endowment support:* This type of funding is given to an organization to begin or to add to its endowment fund. An endowment is a reserve of funds (a recommended 200 percent of the institution's operating budget) that the organization invests in a variety of ways to yield the maximum in interest and dividends. Only the income from investments is used by the organization to pay expenses. If the principal is properly invested, it will provide long-term financial security for the organization. An organization is ready to embark on an endowment campaign only if it has a long-range plan and is financially stable, with an operating cash reserve and solid support from a substantial number of donors plus no accumulated debt. An operating cash reserve (a recommended 25 percent of the budget) is set aside by the institution for special opportunities or emergencies; it can also be used to ease cash-flow problems by borrowing from it rather than a bank, thus avoiding interest payments. A cash reserve should be replenished at the end of each fiscal year and increased in accordance with budgetary growth.

*Matching grants or challenge grants:* These types of grants are awarded on the condition that the dollar amount of the grant will be equaled, or matched, by dollars contributed from other sources. The match can be a direct one-to-one ratio or a multiple of as much as three-to-one. Grants given by the National Endowment for the Arts, for example, are of this type. The "challenge" is made by a funding source to the organization, requiring it to raise a certain amount of funds from other sources to match the funds offered in the challenge grant. Funds provided through matching, or challenge, grants can be earmarked as general, project, capital, or endowment support.

Other types of support, such as bequests and planned giving through life-insurance policies, trusts, annuities, and pooled-income funds, are not, in most cases, part of an annual campaign to fund current operations. To secure these types of gifts, specialized legal and financial expertise is often required.

The typical size of a gift varies widely, depending on the funding source; contribution levels usually relate to the size of the total budget. For example, if a business has a total annual contribution budget of $80,000, a request for a grant of $20,000 would not under normal circumstances be approved. A request for $1,000 to $5,000 would be more appropriate.

It is important to evaluate renewal candidates and new prospects in terms of all the above-mentioned criteria. It is not unusual for a business's giving policies to change from year to year due to changes in personnel, financial performance, and perception of community needs. Individuals also change their philanthropic interests. The information sources that provide the most accurate and useful details are described below. Additional sources are listed in Appendix C.

## Sources for Researching Businesses

*Chamber of commerce:* Information on businesses can be obtained through local chambers of commerce. A working relationship with the chamber of commerce can be invaluable in identifying leaders or important contacts in the business sector and in community affairs.

*Telephone directories:* The Yellow Pages list businesses in specific localities by industry.

*Directory of Directors; Dun & Bradstreet Million Dollar Directory; Dun & Bradstreet Reference Book of Corporate Managements; Moody's Industrial Manual;* and *Standard and Poor's Register of Corporations, Directors, and Executives:* These are standard reference books used by businesses. They list corporate sales figures, top managers, board members, numbers of employees, plant locations, products, divisions, subsidiaries, addresses, and telephone numbers.

*Corporate 500: The Directory of Corporate Philanthropy; Corporate Foundation Profiles; A Guide to Corporate Giving in the Arts;* and the *Taft Corporate Foundation Directory:* These specialized books list general information on corporate support policies, previous grants made, and the appropriate contacts, addresses, and telephone numbers of specific corporations.

## Sources for Researching Foundations

*The Foundation Center:* The Center is a not-for-profit organization with national offices in New York and Washington, D.C., and branches in public libraries throughout the United States. Its purpose is to disseminate information on foundations. The Foundation Center Associates Program provides members with information over the telephone. Several of the Center's most useful directories and information sources are mentioned below.

*The Foundation Directory,* published biannually, contains a comprehensive list of all foundations in America that have assets of at least $1 million or that have awarded total grants of $100,000 or more annually. Each foundation listing includes a description of its grant policies, as well as its address, telephone number, and foundation officers.

*Source Book Profiles* provides in-depth information on the 1,000 largest foundations in America. Examples and amounts of past grants are given, as well as descriptions of the programs and activities the foundation is interested in supporting and the geographic area(s) served by grantees.

*Comsearch Printouts: Subjects* lists foundations making grants of $5,000 or more according to the 50 most popular grant-making interests. The entries are grouped alphabetically by state within the grant categories, listing the names of foundations, their grant recipients and locations, the amounts and dates of grants awarded, and the activities funded.

*Comsearch Printouts: Geographic* arranges the same information included in *Comsearch Printouts: Subjects* by location of recipient organizations rather than by grant categories.

*Internal Revenue Service Information Return*: Form 990PF is kept on file by the Center. All private foundations are required by law to file an annual information return and make it public. Form 990PF indicates the types of activities and organizations a foundation is interested in supporting, listing the amounts awarded as well as the recipients; it also provides information on the financial condition of a foundation, reporting total awards granted, transactions made, and total assets.

*The Foundation Grants Index Annual* provides information on all grants exceeding $5,000 a year. This directory lists foundations alphabetically within each state.

*The National Data Book* briefly describes the nation's 24,000 currently active private foundations.

*The Taft Foundation Directory* lists general information on specific foundations, including examples of grants made by each foundation listed.

State foundation directories describe the foundations operating within a given state. Check with the local library for a particular state's foundation directory. (See Appendix D.)

## Sources for Researching Individuals

*Marquis' Who's Who* and *The Social Register* provide biographical summaries of celebrities and prominent business and community leaders.

*People in Philanthropy* lists individuals who regularly contribute large amounts to charitable organizations.

## Sources for Researching Government Agencies

*The Catalog of Federal Domestic Assistance* is useful to organizations seeking support from the federal government. It describes all federal programs that provide assistance to various entities for programs serving the general public.

Government representatives at the federal, state, and local levels can provide information about obtaining government grants and can be effective intermediaries on behalf of the prospective grantee.

## Sources for General Research

Periodicals such as *Forbes, Fortune, Business Week, Foundation News, The Wall Street Journal,* and *The New York Times,* as well as local newspapers, report information regarding current events and economic trends in the business and philanthropic sectors.

With the increasing use of computers in fundraising, many new research services are available. Some of these provide in-depth information on businesses, individuals, foundations, and general topics in the news, as well as cross-reference an organization's donor, subscription, or membership list against other outside lists (such as directors and trustees of all foundations in the United States), or against the donor lists of other institutions.

Annual reports published by foundations and government agencies provide a record of an agency's philanthropic activity over a year's time. Annual reports typically list the philanthropic mission and the policy on making grants. Examples of grants awarded are usually listed. A corporation's annual report to its stockholders provides very useful information regarding the company's financial performance and outlook and occasionally includes details on philanthropic policies and activities.

## CULTIVATION PLANS

After compiling lists of renewal candidates and new prospects, it must be determined who will share with the development director the responsibility of approaching, or "cultivating," prospective donors. The individuals who will help approach prospective donors on behalf of the cultural organization are called referees. The cultivation plan identifies the methods leading up to the actual request or solicitation.

The list of renewal candidates should be circulated to all board members to determine who among them might know individual donors or the contact person, a trustee, or a top official of the institutional funding sources; such board members can therefore act as referees. This is particularly helpful in cases where the organization is asking a funding source for an increased level of support. It may seem unnecessary to circulate among board members a list of renewal candidates with whom relationships are already established, but this process may uncover stronger contacts and new information. The membership of the organization's board of trustees, as well as an institutional funding source's decision makers, may have changed during the year, and it is important to identify new contacts.

The list of new prospects, which includes the names and addresses of funding sources and in the case of businesses, foundations, and government agencies their top officials, should also be circulated to board members in advance of the campaign and throughout the year as additional prospects are identified. All trustees should indicate those listed individuals whom they know. The development director must then arrange to meet with each board member to discuss how each funding source should be approached—in a personal meeting with a representative of the funding source, through a letter written on personal or business stationery, or through a telephone call—and what the development director's role should be. When appropriate, the managing director and program director should be asked to participate in solicitations.

The development director should make the solicitation process easy for board members and senior staff by drafting all appeal letters for their approval and by preparing accompanying materials and setting up appointments. Once the referees and cultivation plans have been determined, the development director must make certain that all referees receive the proper information and back-up materials and that all carry out their responsibilities.

## SOLICITING THE FUNDING SOURCE

When the development director has determined the fundraising approach, or cultivation plan, the actual solicitation of the gift can take place. The solicitation process usually involves the following steps: telephone call is made, an introductory letter is sent (see Appendix I, "Introductory Letter") or a proposal package is submitted, and a face-to-face meeting takes place. The solicitation process is frequently not as formal when requesting funds from individuals.

### Introductory Telephone Call or Letter

To initiate the solicitation process, the development director usually makes a telephone call directly to the funding source. This call, often made to an assistant or secretary, informs the funding source that a request for funds will be submitted. The call also allows the development director to verify basic information about the individual or agency, such as correct spellings of names and to whom to write. This call should be kept brief—it is not a substitute for in-depth research. If for some reason the funding source cannot be reached on the telephone, it is appropriate to write a letter. In the case of individuals, the solicitation process is often initiated by the referee rather than by the development director.

### Proposal Package

The proposal package is made up of a covering letter, the proposal, and accompanying materials. The covering letter should be written to the individual prospect, to the grants officer or president, or to whoever has been identified as the appropriate contact person at the business or foundation. This letter should briefly mention the nature of the particular request and describe the accompanying materials. If the grant request is to a past contributor, a statement of thanks for past support should be mentioned. Often, when requesting general operating support, all of the items normally included in the proposal and the covering letter are incorporated into one appeal letter.

The proposal should:

- Introduce the organization and state its purpose and mission.
- Indicate why the organization is unique and worthy of support from the particular funding source.
- Describe, briefly, the project or general program of the organization for which funds are being requested.
- Cite some of the organization's program highlights; the audience, attendance, or participation figures; positive critical reviews; and associations with notable people.
- Mention briefly a few of the organization's major current donors. This serves as an endorsement of the organization and may enhance the organization's credibility with the particular funding source. This concept is more helpful with new prospects and may not be necessary when dealing with a source familiar with the institution. A complete list of donors is typically included as an attachment to the proposal.
- Make the request for funds. Ask for an appropriate amount of money, which has been determined through prior research. Indicate the impact of the potential contribution on the organization; if applicable, mention the public relations advantages or employee benefits, such as credits on promotional materials, free admission, discount tickets, special events or ticket hotline service, available to the funding source in return for its support.
- Indicate that a follow-up call will be made in about a week by the development director to make sure the proposal has been received and to set up a meeting or to offer an invitation to attend a performance or tour the facilities.

Generally, the proposal should be concise, no longer than two or three pages. A lengthy proposal will most likely not be read due to the vast amount of mail received by the funding source. When a major project is being developed with a funding source, an in-depth proposal may be requested, which will require more detail and a more lengthy presentation. The proposal should present the organization in the most professional and organized manner possible. It should be accurately typewritten and easy to read. See Appendix I, "Corporate General-Support Renewal Proposal," "Corporate Special Project Proposal," and "Foundation Special Project Proposal," for examples of some proposals.

The materials accompanying the proposal should be the specific pieces of background information that most funding sources need in order to make their funding decisions. The following items should accompany requests:

- Overall organizational budget and, if requesting special-project support, individual project budgets (clear, comprehensive budgets are essential to the proposal package—see charts 3.6 and 3.7 for examples of budget formats.)

## CHART 3.6 ORGANIZATIONAL BUDGET

---

DATE

**REVENUE**
Ticket Sales                                    $
Parking Lot Concession
Hall Rentals
Concessions and Other Income
Advertising Sales
Touring Fees

                              Sub-Total    $ _____

**PUBLIC AND PRIVATE SUPPORT**

**Private**
Foundations                                     $
Businesses
Individuals
- Patrons
- Lower Level
Special Events (net)

**Public**
Federal
State
Municipal

                              Sub-Total    $ _____
           TOTAL ALL INCOME    $ _____

**EXPENSES**
Program                                         $
Administration
Interest
Parking Lot
Equipment Rental
Rent
Utilities

                              Sub-Total    $ _____
       TOTAL ALL EXPENSES    $ _____

---

- Brief history of the institution and statement of future plans
- List of donors from the previous fiscal year
- IRS 501(c)(3) tax exempt identification letter

- List of board members and their professional affiliations
- Schedule of programs taking place during the year
- Most recent audited financial statement
- Most recent annual report
- Illustrative materials, such as brochures, newspaper clippings, and magazine reprints

## CHART 3.7 PROGRAM BUDGET

DATE

### (New Theatrical Production)

**EXPENSES**
Commissioning Fees                                                                $
Performers' Fees
Stagehands
Wardrobe
Advertising and Promotion
Legal and Insurance
Box Office
Ushers
Maintenance and Security
Mail-Order House
Postage
Instrument Tuning
Administrative and Benefits*
Printing

                    TOTAL ALL EXPENSES     $ _____

**INCOME**

**Earned**
Ticket Sales                                                                              $

**Public and Private Support**
(List actual sources if known)

**Private**
Businesses
Foundations
Individuals

**Public**
Federal
State
Municipal

                    TOTAL ALL INCOME     $ _____
Amount Remaining to be Raised                                         $
Amount Requested from (name of source)                       $

*Percentage of total administrative costs allocated to this program.

These documents should accompany most requests made during the campaign. The history and plans, donor list, board list, and program schedule should be accurately typed on the organization's letterhead and reproduced in quantity by offset printing. If information in these documents changes significantly, they should be updated and reprinted. It is also important not to inundate the funding source with reviews, brochures, and other publicity materials. Instead, it is best to send only the most significant documents.

## The Meeting

The meeting is of primary importance to the success of the funding request. Because of the enormous number of requests and even greater number of persons trying to contact funding sources, it can be difficult to make appointments with them. It is important, however, to pursue an appointment and to establish a working relationship with the funding-source contact. Making the call to request an appointment is one of the hardest parts of a fundraiser's job. The referee can be extremely helpful in securing the appointment either by making the call directly or by allowing the development director to mention his or her name. When making a cold call, refer to the introductory letter or proposal and explain that a meeting is the best way to convey the impact of the project and its compatibility with the funding source's grant-making objectives as well as to gain the source's input.

Once an appointment has been made, the development director must be prepared to present the organization as a programmatically significant and administratively sound organization. The following points should be kept in mind when meeting with the funding source:

- Be on time for the appointment.
- Begin the discussion by reiterating the goals of the organization and then explain the administrative structure that backs up the programmatic aims.
- Do not waste the person's time with an overlong recital of the organization's record of achievement. Take time to listen; this is a chance to hear directly from the source how funding decisions are made.
- It may make sense to include other appropriate representatives of the organization at this meeting—perhaps the program director or managing director or a board member. Usually no more than three persons from the organization should attend. These representatives must be well informed and articulate and must contribute to the meeting.
- As soon as possible after the meeting, the development director should write to thank the person for taking the time to meet.

- If the request for funds results in a grant, a thank you letter and official receipt should be sent shortly after the funds are received; if denied a grant, send a note of appreciation for considering the proposal.

## BUILDING A SENSE OF OWNERSHIP

Successful fundraising requires that the organization's leaders build a sense of shared ownership among the staff, board of trustees, audience, donors, and community at large.

By instilling a sense of ownership in actual and prospective donors, the organization can enhance the likelihood of receiving contributions and grants and of having them renewed in subsequent years. A sense of ownership can be developed through thoughtful donor services, such as newsletters, priority ticket services, and receptions. Certainly, all donors should be included on the organization's general mailing list, and information should be sent to them on a regular basis about performances, programs, exhibitions, and special events.

Keeping donors informed is one of the most important, though often neglected, activities in the fundraising campaign. In order to sustain their interest and encourage their involvement, donors should be kept aware of new activities and programs, new appointments to the board, staff changes, and grants received. Newsletters (see Appendix I, "Newsletters"), donor magazines, and press releases are excellent vehicles for conveying this information.

Donors should also be invited to performances, exhibitions, screenings, and lectures/demonstrations. There is no more effective way for a donor or prospective new donor to become involved in the organization than by experiencing firsthand the activities of the organization. Complimentary tickets, VIP seating, and priority subscriptions are extra benefits that can be made available to donors.

Special premium packages can be developed for donors at various contribution levels. Premiums may include use of a VIP lounge at performances; invitations to special receptions; discounts on tickets and boutique items; offers of merchandise such as tote bags, books, or records; or subscriptions to a newsletter or magazine.

Special premiums can also be developed for employees of corporations contributing at a specified level; premiums may include discounts on merchandise and tickets or free parking and admission passes for the employee's entire family. It is important to make sure that merchandise and services are not given away too cheaply and that delivering them efficiently to donors will not require an excessive amount of staff time.

It is also important to communicate with donors in ways other than requesting funds. The organization should express appreciation to donors for their generosity at every opportunity, for example, by sending them Christmas cards, or giving them souvenir booklets and anniversary programs that list their names.

An annual report should also be produced at the end of each fiscal year and made available to both donors and the general public. The annual report is the organization's external statement of its financial and programmatic performance during the preceding year. The report should summarize the organization's activities and management practices, reporting the amount of funds raised, the donors, and the manner in which the funds were spent. The organization's audited financial statements should also be included. Every organization, no matter how small, should produce an annual report. The annual report need not be a glossy four-color book in order to give an effective presentation of the organization's achievements over the prior year. See Appendix I, "Annual Report," for an example of an annual report.

## THE COMPUTER AND FUNDRAISING

The computer is an absolute boon to fundraising with many applications beyond the obvious one of storing donor records. The computer can help the fundraiser do everything from setting goals to building a sense of ownership in donors, from approaching all types of prospects to managing special events. The trick is to make the computer work on the organization's behalf rather than overwhelm it. Computerized information that is accurate, timely, and presented in easy-to-use report formats will result in greatly increased procedural efficiency, decision-making effectiveness, and fundraising success.

This section will explain ways to use the computer for fundraising. Four sections are covered and presented in increasing order of sophistication:

- Word processing
- Desktop publishing
- Record keeping
- Campaign analysis, goal setting, and targeting

The technical aspects of operating, converting, or installing computers will not be covered in this book; they are subjects best left to computer experts.

## Word Processing

The word-processing function of a computer is usually the first operation that someone new to computers learns. It makes sense to novices because it seems like a glorified typewriter. It is, in fact, a great deal more than that.

It is incredibly helpful in writing proposals and producing all the standard proposal back-up materials mentioned in the section on the proposal package earlier in this chapter. The beauty of the computer is that one can input a basic document, then revise and tailor it as necessary depending on the source to which it is being sent. Funding sources often ask how a particular program meets their own funding guidelines. Since each source has its own peculiar guidelines, it is easy to flesh out or pare down various sections of a proposal to satisfy these differences. It is possible to have three or four versions of each of the program proposals for which the fundraiser is seeking funds during a particular fiscal year, each designed for a different donor market.

Most proposals, regardless of their subjects, contain information that needs to appear in every proposal, such as a brief history of the organization. These items need be input only once, then transferred into each new proposal. This cuts down enormously on proofreading as well as inputting time.

Developing a standard introductory letter is easy. As mentioned earlier, many sources wish to have preliminary information on an organization before granting an appointment. By having an "intro" letter on the computer, one can tailor the opening line to the precise telephone conversation that took place, such as "Your secretary, Joan Brown, suggested that I send you some background information on XYZ Program in preparation for our 10:00 a.m. meeting on January 15, 1989."

It is very important to develop a system to name the documents in a descriptive way so that they can be easily retrieved later. Instead of naming a proposal document for the source, such as the XYZ Foundation proposal, name it for the information it contains that may need to be retrieved later for inclusion in another proposal. For example, assume a generic proposal has been developed for an arts-education project. This version could be named "Arts Ed—Gen." It is likely that sources supporting the public schools, as well as those interested specifically in increasing awareness of the arts in the community, may be interested in it. Two versions may be developed, one emphasizing the needs of the schools and how the arts-education project will meet them, the other emphasizing the impact of bringing the arts into the schools; name the former "Arts Ed—Ed" and the latter "Arts Ed—Arts."

Another feature of the computer is its ability to produce personalized appeal letters. The word-processing function, together with list processing or data processing, allows you to develop a letter (word processing) and insert in it selected information from the donor records (list processing or data processing), such as the name of the program you wish the donor to fund, the amount of the previous year's gift, and the amount requested for the current campaign. Thus the appeal letters are mass produced but individually tailored to each source—a method as efficient as it is effective.

## Desktop Publishing

With the development of desktop publishing functions, computers can also be used to set type, design graphics, create charts and tables, compose and lay out a page, and merge text with graphics. This enables the development office to create newsletters and invitations to receptions, special lectures, and forums, thus keeping donors informed about and involved in the organization. Proposals can also be enhanced by including charts and tables that can present information more clearly and easily than in text. Even without desktop publishing capabilities, invitations in letter form as well as simple one-page newsletters can be produced as an easy and fast way to communicate with donors.

## Record Keeping

The data-processing and record-keeping functions of computers are the heart of a fundraising campaign. This is where all the information from the manual record-keeping system outlined earlier in this chapter is stored: the principal record file, aspects of the current campaign tracking folder, the campaign status report, the research profiles, and the contribution-processing file. The information is found in a series of "screens" for each particular donor. Please refer to Chart 3.8 for an explanation of how information from a manual system is used in a computer system. Typical screens include:

- Principal record
- Funding history
- Research profile
- Current campaign tracking

It is a good idea to have the computer system in the development office integrated with the system used in the accounting office; in this way, gifts received have to be input only once to appear in both the accounting system and the donor records. This cuts down on error and minimizes the tedious task of verifying and balancing entries.

Another important integration feature is the ability of linking individual donor files with foundation or corporate donor files. This is important when a top official of a company is also a personal contributor. For example, when soliciting or acknowledging renewal of the individual's gift, it is wise to thank the individual for the corporate contribution as well.

## CHART 3.8 PRACTICAL USES OF COMPUTERIZED RECORDS

| RECORD | EXAMPLES OF REPORTS AND DOCUMENTS PRODUCED |
|---|---|
| A. Principal Record File | Headings and salutations for letters and invitations; Mailing labels and envelopes; Rolodex cards; List of corporate donors within a defined geographic area. |
| B. Funding History | Receipts and thank you letters; Mailing labels of donors over $50 who are eligible to receive a tote bag; List of donors who supported a particular project; List of donors to be renewed in June; List of donors who purchased benefit tickets; Campaign support plan summaries. |
| C. Research Profile | Profiles on prospects as preparation for a fundraising call; List of donors and prospects with a particular program interest; List of donors and prospects who used to be board members; List of prospects by referee; List of donors who attended a special reception. |
| D. Current Campaign Tracking | List of donors still needing to be renewed with appeal letter "B"; List of foundations that have February proposal deadlines; List of donors needing progress reports in June. |

With all this information linked in the computer and with a system of coding that enables the operator to select by certain variables, the number of reports and lists that the development director can create is almost endless. These include lists of donors and prospects, mailing labels, rolodex address cards, a month by month calendar of appeal dates, monthly campaign status reports, or donor profiles as preparation for a board member's fundraising calls.

The variety of lists alone that can be produced makes the computer a priceless addition to the development department. Some useful lists and their applications include:

- Lapsed donors segregated by the special project previously supported. For example, there might have been a past effort to raise funds for a special jazz series and the organization wants to launch another jazz event. Simply generate a list of lapsed donors who supported this kind of activity in the past. Time can be saved by not having to research a list of prospects with interests in jazz. A quick letter can be written and merged with this list of lapsed donors.

- Names of funding sources known by a particular board member that have not renewed their gifts at the halfway point in the campaign. A reminder letter can be composed for the board member's signature and merged with this list.

- Names of all donors and prospects with an interest in a special program who live in a particular city. This might be useful if the organization is going to be holding a reception to celebrate a new program. An invitation letter can be composed and merged with this list. A list of invitees with addresses and phone numbers can then be generated to keep track of RSVPs.
- A list of all lower level givers whose gift anniversary date falls in a particular month of the current fiscal year. This group of donors should be sent a renewal letter several months in advance of their anniversary date.

This discussion is not meant to be all-inclusive, only to give an idea of the endless applications of computer technology in fundraising. Please refer to Chart 3.9 for additional considerations in selecting and using a computer.

A crucial aspect of all these functions is to make sure that the computer operator is able to sort the data in the most useful ways. Give a great deal of thought to this. Another potential problem to guard against is "dirty data," i.e., inaccurate data. Care needs to be taken in the input phase to ensure that categories of information are well defined and that the inputter is accurate and understands the categories.

**CHART 3.9 COMPUTER FUNDRAISING SYSTEM CHECKLIST**

1. Think five years ahead and quantify the number of donors, the number of gifts, pledges, planned gifts, and events, the staff and processing organization expects to have.
2. Don't be too price conscious—penny wise, pound foolish.
3. What do you need the computer to do; list your current needs then think about automatic gift processing, recording pledges, letter quality printing.
4. Ask specific questions, such as how long will it take to run 150 letters or process 150 gifts.
5. Can the printer easily accommodate different size stationery, can it be put on feed?
6. Do envelopes have to be inserted manually to print?
7. Make sure information system is integrated. Only through an integrated system where all information on a donor is available to you can one build solid relationships of trust, the very bedrock of fundraising.
8. Can you use letter codes instead of number codes, and can you define your own codes? Avoid donor record systems that require you to input a code for each donor.
9. Are you limited in your name and address fields?
10. Can you sort by what you need to sort by?

## Campaign Analysis, Goal Setting, and Targeting

At the completion of a fundraising campaign, an analysis can be conducted that tells the development director how much money was raised from various strategies, how many donors renewed or increased their gifts, how many new donors were acquired as well as other important facts. This information can form the basis of the goal-setting exercise for the next year's campaign and help define strategies.

The targeting of hot, warm, and cold prospects can also be done on the computer. The following variables are strong determinants of whether a source is a hot prospect:

- Degree to which giving interests and geographical scope mesh with organization's programs
- Degree of referee-contact relationship—how close the relationship is and how much decision-making power the contact has
- Degree to which funds are available and the economic condition of source is strong

Once the variables are determined for measuring the potential of a prospect (and many other ones can be added to those listed above), the development director should rate each prospect numerically against each variable. A numerical rating system of 1 to 5 can be employed for each prospect, with 5 being the hottest. The prospects with the highest number of points, say 15 if only three variables are used, should be approached in the first month of the campaign, and those that score the lowest should be left until the end of the campaign or not pursued at all.

# Chapter 4
# Business

Business, recognizing the important work done by not-for-profit organizations in America, has supported health, education, and welfare causes to varying degrees since the 1940s. It was not until the 1970s, however, that businesses began to contribute to arts and culture in a sizable way. The Business Committee for the Arts reported that in 1967 businesses contributed $22 million to the arts and that by 1982 the figure had risen to $506 million.

While philanthropy from the business sector has increased over the years, it still represents only 5.2 percent of total charitable contributions. Contributions from businesses to all causes totaled $4.5 billion in 1986. Culture receives approximately 11 cents of every corporate contribution dollar, with education receiving 38 cents; health and welfare, 29 cents; civic activities, 17 cents; and all other causes, 5 cents.

According to the American Association of Fund-Raising Counsel, Inc., only a portion, 30 percent, of all U.S. corporations made any contributions at all in 1986 and only 9.1 percent were responsible for giving over 50 percent of all corporate support. This latter group includes most of the nation's largest corporations, the segment that has been most affected by the recent wave of mergers, acquisitions, and general corporate downsizing.

In the nonprofit sector, arts and cultural groups must compete with health, education, and welfare organizations for a share of the corporate largess. Support given to cultural programs, however, can often provide a business far greater visibility and prestige than support given to other charitable causes. In order to secure corporate grants, cultural organizations must educate businesses in their communities about the benefits to be derived. To involve businesses in supporting arts and cultural organizations, an organization's development personnel must understand:

- Why businesses support arts and culture
- What determines the giving policy of businesses
- How businesses make funding decisions

- What kind of support is available
- How to approach businesses for support

## WHY BUSINESS SUPPORTS ARTS AND CULTURE

Businesses support arts and culture for sound business reasons in addition to altruistic ones. A firm's operations and its ability to earn a profit are often improved through involvement in and support of the community in which it does business. An arts and cultural organization offers services that directly benefit a corporation's customers, clients, and employees. A thriving cultural community can help a business recruit and retain highly educated and talented personnel, as well as significantly spur economic development by attracting people to visit theaters, galleries, museums, restaurants, and shops. Arts and culture are generally viewed as positive forces, promoting goodwill among customers, clients, employees, and throughout a community.

For all of these reasons, businesses tend to contribute to cultural organizations in communities where they have headquarters, major markets, plants, or branch offices. A recent survey of 500 corporations conducted by the American Council on the Arts showed that 87 percent deemed geographical location the most important criterion when selecting grant recipients.

Corporate managements recognize the public-relations value in supporting culture. By underwriting such programs, a business identifies itself with artistic and cultural excellence and adds a human element to its corporate image. Additionally, businesses benefit enormously from supporting popular productions, exhibitions, and national television programs. The rationale is simple: The more people who see these programs, the more people there will be who think positively of the program's corporate sponsor.

Businesses also receive a tax savings by contributing to charitable causes. The Internal Revenue Service allows businesses to deduct contributions up to 10 percent of their adjusted net income. However, it appears that this tax advantage is not the major incentive for businesses to contribute to charity.

## WHAT DETERMINES A BUSINESS'S GIVING POLICY?

A business's giving policy—the amount of funds it allocates to various types of charitable causes—is a reflection of its markets, products, image, earnings, and, in general, its way of doing business. Industries such as commercial banks and utilities, which are dependent on large consumer markets, tend to give highly visible support to a broad range of organizations. In contrast, a manufacturing firm selling to a wholesale market may give little, if anything, to arts and culture.

Many businesses like to target support directly to their major or developing markets. For instance, the primary market of a national fast-food chain is children. As a result, this business supports a series of children's concerts performed by local symphony orchestras in communities it serves.

A business's product line can often influence where it directs its philanthropic support. Pharmaceutical firms, for example, may direct their funds entirely to programs in the health field. A high-technology corporation, on the other hand, may allot its charitable budget to educational programs in engineering and the sciences. During the latter half of the 1970s and early 1980s the large oil companies as a group spent millions of dollars annually to sponsor programs on national television that helped promote favorable public opinion.

The earnings profile of a company also affects its giving policy. The size of a business's philanthropic contribution budget is generally based on profits earned during the previous year. If earnings are off, contributions may be held at the level of the preceding year or cut back.

In recent years the incredible spate of mergers and acquisitions has reduced the number of corporations contributing to charity. This activity has had both positive and negative effects on charity in the United States. For example, the takeover and subsequent closing of the dominant corporate employer in a community virtually eliminates that community's major contributions. On the other hand, a takeover can invigorate an otherwise sagging operation and provide new and increasing support.

Cultural organizations must analyze each corporate prospect individually in terms of its markets, products, image, and earnings. By approaching businesses with this thorough knowledge, as equals rather than as supplicants, arts and cultural organizations can establish business partnerships with corporations. In exchange for funding support, an organization can provide a business valuable public relations opportunities, improved market or product identification, and, in some cases, increased revenue.

## HOW BUSINESSES MAKE FUNDING DECISIONS

A business's decision to fund a cultural organization depends on many criteria and is often several years in the making. Support awarded beyond the token level is typically a result of judgments made by the business about its own interests and needs.

A business that makes a grant to an organization will have researched it. A business's first requirement is that the organization be a not-for-profit, tax-exempt corporation. Other important factors considered in making a funding decision are the level of referee contacts, the professional qualifications of the board of trustees and management staff, the makeup of its audience or client group, the state of its finances, and its participation figures. Ultimately, the business will give to those organizations that are the most credible, the most relevant to its interests, and of the highest quality.

## WHAT KIND OF SUPPORT IS AVAILABLE?

Business support to culture and the arts is generally of five types:

- General support
- Special project support
- Service-in-kind support
- Employee matching gift program
- Special-event support

### General Support

Grants to help cover the operating expenses of an organization usually range from $500 to $10,000. This money is typically paid out of a business's annual contribution budget. It can take three years of repeated appeals to a likely prospect before a general support grant is received. Once an organization has received a grant, it is much easier to receive support in subsequent years. A request for support must be made every year, regardless of whether the organization is included as a line item in the business's annual contribution budget.

### Special Project Support

Special project grants, such as sponsorship of a play or art exhibition, tend to be larger—$10,000 to $50,000 or more—than general-support grants and may come, in part or in total, from a business's advertising or public affairs budget. These types of grants are becoming increasingly popular in the corporate sector and are viewed by sponsors not only as philanthropy but as a way to enhance a sponsor's image or income. As the special project's sponsor, the business can acquire public relations benefits when its name is directly attached to the project and publicized through brochures and television and print advertising. The essence of the sponsorship concept is to give the corporation maximum visibility and identification with the project.

When seeking a sponsor for a special project, the cultural organization must attempt to match the project's expected audience with a business that has a similar customer profile and similar demographics. For example, a bank dealing with an upscale clientele may be an appropriate sponsor for a chamber music series. A corporate sponsor wishing to be known as adventuresome and innovative may sponsor avant-garde events or exhibitions featuring contemporary painting. A corporation with international business interests may wish to sponsor a project featuring arts and culture from areas of the world where they have a corporate presence. The idea of enlightened corporate self-interest can guide the development director's research for sponsors.

The arts organization must then work with the corporation to design a sponsorship package that is mutually beneficial. Because of the nature of sponsorships, the business will want to be very involved in many publicity and marketing decisions associated with the project. The more creative the partnership between the nonprofit organization and the sponsor, the more impact the sponsorship will have.

A comprehensive sponsorship of a series of plays, for example, might include:

1. *Credits package*: A written credit line, such as "The ABC play series has been sponsored by a grant from the XYZ Corporation," should appear on all printed material developed for the project, including brochures, newspaper ads of a reasonable size, and the house program. The credit should be large enough to be noticed, but not overwhelming, and can include the corporate logo. Credits can also be extended to include an article about the sponsorship or an ad recognizing the sponsor in the program or institution's newsletter. If media ads are purchased on radio or television, sponsor credits can also be included, provided enough time and space are available.

2. *Events*: The sponsor should be given a pre-negotiated number of complimentary tickets to the opening night and other nights throughout the run of the show. If the sponsor wishes large numbers of tickets, they should be sold to the company with some discount. For example, the arts organization may offer 20 complimentary seats to the opening for the chief executive office and the corporation's top clients, 4 free tickets to each additional night, and all other tickets at a 20 percent discount. Naturally, the sponsor should be given good seat locations.

   Alternatively (or additionally) the cultural organization could offer to host an employee's night, when the corporation would bring a large group to the performance (purchasing their tickets at a discount) and the organization would provide complimentary wine and cheese at intermission. Sometimes the corporation may wish to host a small, private dinner for its guests with the artistic director of the institution after a performance. The development director should work with a staff person at the corporation on all plans for the event and be as helpful as possible. The corporation should pay for the dinner in addition to their sponsorship grant, unless it has already been agreed that events such as this are the arts organization's financial responsibility. If an opening-night party takes place, the sponsor should be verbally acknowledged and thanked publicly at the event; sometimes top corporate officials can be designated as guests of honor.

It is important to be flexible and creative when developing the package of sponsor benefits. A sponsor may wish to put a small exhibition of its products in the lobby, insert information in the program, offer a special coupon or premium to members of the audience, do a special mailing to all of the members of the institution, or add a "stuffer" to their monthly bills to customers. The arts organization and the sponsor should be cooperative but careful not to become too commercial and overstep the boundaries of good taste, thereby undoing the goodwill that is the basis of the sponsorship.

In some cases, a business will develop a cause-related marketing effort with an organization, i.e., a sponsorship concept designed to tie corporate income to a designated project. For example, every time an individual uses a certain kind of credit card to buy a ticket, that credit card company will donate a specific amount of money to the institution.

Affinity credit cards (cards that are tied to a specific institution or theme; see Appendix I, "Affinity Card Mailing") are another example of this kind of *quid pro quo* relationship between a sponsor and an institution. The affinity card concept works in the following way: A bank works with an institution to design a credit card that features the logo or message of the institution. The bank then writes a letter over the signature of the organization's head to its members or ticket buyers to let them know that every time the card is used a certain percentage of the bank's fee will be donated to the institution. In this way, individuals who believe in the institution have yet another opportunity to offer support at no additional cost to themselves. The institution is the recipient of additional funds, and the bank has many new customers. This relationship has the potential to benefit everyone, but the arts organization must also be aware that it is obligated to one bank exclusively and cannot run similar programs with competitive credit card companies. It also must be made clear to the organization's members that this is an additional way to help the organization and should not replace the individual's annual donation.

Since the concept of sponsorship is both a way to generate larger grants and develop higher visibility, the development director should focus on how to take program plans and develop them into special projects. For example, an institution could seek a sponsor for a series of plays or a sponsor for each production. A membership drive could be sponsored, or even a series of institutional ads. A wine company could provide wine for all institutional events over the course of the season and thus be designated the "house wine" of the institution. In other words, the development director must provide opportunities for donors to be identified and associated with a particular aspect of the institution's program.

If a project is large and too expensive for a single sponsor, the development director could develop a consortium sponsorship and seek out compatible corporations to sponsor a project collectively. For example, a real-estate developer and a bank might agree to be partners, whereas two banks might not. Sometimes the possibility of the right partnership might be even more attractive to a potential donor than an exclusive sponsorship.

In most every case, corporate sponsors will allow the institution to supplement their donations with foundation and government funds.

## Service-in-Kind Support

Service-in-kind support is a donation of business services, as opposed to money, at little extra cost to the business. Donations may include used furniture and equipment; office, rehearsal, or exhibit space; printing and design, word processing, or other professional services. For example, lobby space in a business may be offered to a visual arts organization to use as an exhibition area. This expands the gallery space of the organization and brings in a wider audience, serving the interests of both the business and the arts organization.

The value of donated services to organizations can often be far greater than the amount of a cash grant. Some businesses, however, have policies prohibiting donations of their products, while others like to provide samples of such products as perfume or liquor to large gatherings of people at special events. Small local businesses are good prospects for in-kind services and will often participate in special events such as street fairs. It is often easier for them to provide in-kind support than to make cash grants. The development director should review the organization's annual expense budget to look for items that can be contributed in-kind, thus saving the organization from having to purchase them.

## Employee Matching Gift Programs

An employee matching gift program provides a way for businesses to contribute to the arts while also giving their employees an incentive to contribute. It works this way: A business makes a gift to an organization to "match" the contribution already donated by one of the business's employees. The business donation can equal the employee's, or the matching ratio can be even greater, depending on the policy of the individual business. For example, an employee contributes $100 to a local museum and registers the gift with the matching gift program of the employing firm which has a policy of matching employee gifts on a two-to-one basis. The museum receives a total of $300. Most businesses set some restrictions on the type of not-for-profit organizations it contributes to, as well as on the size of gifts that are eligible for matching funds.

Because employees sometimes fail to report their contributions to the firm's matching gift program, the organization should try to follow up on possible matching gifts. Requesting the individual's business affiliation on the organization's donor pledge card helps in the follow-up process. The organization can then follow up on possible matching gifts by including with the thank you note mailed to donors a small brochure listing the names of businesses known to have matching gift programs. The brochure reminds donors to register their gifts with their employers. The Business Committee for the Arts in New York City publishes a list of matching gift programs, as does the Council on the Advancement and Support of Education in Washington, D.C.

## Special Event Support

Many businesses have funds earmarked to support special events in the community, such as benefit dinners, opening nights, parties, testimonials, and balls. Businesses may purchase blocks of tickets, underwrite the event's expenses, or donate goods. Special events are another way to involve businesses in the activities of arts and cultural organizations.

## HOW TO APPROACH BUSINESSES FOR FUNDS

Most businesses have no formalized giving policies or structures for disbursing funds for philanthropic purposes. Often the special interests and commitment to social responsibility of the chief executive officer are decisive in determining the giving policies of a particular firm. In businesses in which the philanthropic function is well established, such contributions are often within the purview of a specific department in the firm, such as public affairs, community relations, personnel, or corporate communications.

The surest entree into a business is to approach the chief executive officer through a personal friend or business colleague. Board members of cultural organizations are key intermediaries ("referees") in approaching top-level executives. The development director should identify business contacts and personal contacts of each board member to determine if a member knows a top official in the firm in question (see the section on cultivation plans in Chapter 3). After being contacted, the top official of the business, if interested, will make the appropriate staff person aware of the request. The staff person will then handle the ongoing details relating to the request. It is important that the development director establish a relationship with this staff person and include him or her in the solicitation process.

If no personal contacts exist between the board members or senior managers of the organization and the executives of the targeted firm, the development director should determine the staff person responsible for contributions by researching the firm thoroughly; then a telephone call should be made to determine if and when a request for funds is appropriate.

When the time comes to submit a grant request, be sure to tailor it to the firm being approached. The request should be short and concise; it should contain an appropriate request for funds based on research and on information received at the exploratory meeting with the firm's representative. As discussed in Chapter 3, some funding sources will want to receive a request for funds before agreeing to a meeting. The request should include a persuasive presentation of the benefits to the business of providing support and should be mailed with accompanying background materials.

Businesses in which philanthropic giving is an established practice use several different grant-making structures to disburse funds. The most common are:

- Corporate contribution programs
- Corporate foundations
- Advertising and/or public relations departments

Some businesses use all of these structures, sometimes combining them. An understanding of these structures and their interrelationships within a business will aid the development director in identifying the individual in charge of charitable giving and in determining how the approach should be made.

## Corporate Contribution Programs

The corporate contribution program is, in most cases, under the auspices of the public affairs, public relations, or community service department. It may also be administered out of the chief executive's office. Large businesses with national operations often allow branch offices to manage their own contribution budgets under general guidelines determined at corporate headquarters.

Contribution programs are typically managed by one or two persons who are responsible for dealing with requests from all types of not-for-profit groups, including arts and cultural organizations. In some businesses, administering the contribution program is only a part of one person's job. Contribution officers are often overworked because of inadequate back-up staff and may have only a rudimentary knowledge of the arts and culture field. Most contribution officers work closely with a contribution committee made up of executives of the firm. This committee formulates the business's giving policy, establishes the total annual contribution budget, and determines specific grants.

## Corporate Foundations

A corporate foundation is a legal entity established by a corporation as separate from the business. The funds that the foundation disburses annually, however, are obtained from the corporation and can depend on its earnings. The corporation often influences the foundation's giving policies. As is the case with corporate contribution programs, corporate foundations are usually managed by small staffs that work with a board of trustees—similar to the committee overseeing the corporate contribution program—to determine policies and grantees.

## Advertising and/or Public Relations Departments

The advertising and/or public relations department may also disburse funds to not-for-profit organizations. However, these funds are often treated as a business expense and are used to cover advertising, public relations, promotions, and costs associated with special projects and events. These departmental budgets tend to have more discretionary funds available than corporate contribution or corporate foundation budgets. A cultural organization may receive general support funds from a corporation contribution program or a corporate foundation and also receive funds from the corporations public relations or advertising budget to cover a special project and associated advertising.

# Chapter 5
# Foundations

A foundation is a not-for-profit organization established to enrich the public welfare primarily by making grants to social welfare, educational, and health organizations, and to the arts and culture, as well as to other charitable causes. The modern American foundation has been in existence since the early part of this century. The Carnegie Corporation and the Rockefeller Foundation were established in 1911 and 1913, respectively. Today, there are nearly 25,000 foundations operating in the United States, many of them established after World War II.

Through the years foundation support has overwhelmingly gone to educational organizations and health and social welfare causes. The first foundations to support arts and culture resulted from the specific interests of wealthy families, such as the Mellons and Rockefellers. The Andrew Mellon Foundation, established in 1930 as the Mellon Trust, has through the years made grants totaling over $70 million to the National Gallery of Art in Washington, D.C. The Mellon Foundation continues to be a leading donor to many arts organizations throughout the United States. The Rockefeller family was also a major philanthropist in the arts field early on, and the Rockefeller Foundation remains a very visible presence in support of the arts and culture today.

It was not until 1957 that the arts began to attract broad-based foundation support. In that year, the Ford Foundation, through the initiative of W. McNeil Lowry, began an extensive program of support to performing arts organizations, serving as a catalyst for other foundations to support the arts. During the 1960s and 1970s, the Ford Foundation disbursed more than $250 million to the arts and humanities alone, helping theater, dance, music, and opera groups throughout the country to flourish.

Contributions from foundations to all causes totaled $5.17 billion in 1986, which represents only 5.9 percent of all philanthropic contributions. Education, health, and social welfare programs still received the greatest share—66 percent—of foundation grants. In 1985 arts programs received 14.6 percent of foundation funding.

The number of not-for-profit organizations seeking foundation support has steadily increased. As reported in *Foundation Fundamentals,* one million requests for funds are made annually to foundations. Of these requests, no more than 7 percent obtain the support they seek. However, many of the programs for which foundation support is denied are clearly outside the defined interest areas of the foundations.

Arts organizations can increase their chances of receiving funding from foundations by researching prospects carefully and by understanding the following:

- How foundations operate
- What determines the giving policies of foundations
- What kind of support is available
- How to approach foundations for support
- How foundations make funding decisions

## HOW FOUNDATIONS OPERATE

A foundation is established by an initial gift of money from a principal donor or donors. The money is then invested—in stocks, bonds, or real estate, for example—and generates income. The distribution of a foundation's funds is regulated by the Internal Revenue Service, which requires that a minimum amount of funds be paid out annually in grants. The minimum payout is 5 percent of the foundation's assets in each taxable fiscal year.

Of the approximately 25,000 foundations operating in America, 19,000 have assets over $1 million, but only 3,200 make grants in excess of $100,000 annually. There are six major types of foundations. The first four types listed are generally grouped together as independent foundations:

1. *Proprietary foundations*: In this type of foundation, the actual donor—or donor's spouse—is active in the foundation's activities. A proprietary foundation distributes funds according to the interests of the donor, which determine whether there is a specific program focus.
2. *Family foundations*: In a family foundation, policy is determined by family members, usually siblings, children, or grandchildren of the original donor. Grants from this type of foundation follow the original donor's interests, but the family may interpret such interests more broadly. A variation on this type of foundation is the "hybrid family foundation," in which nonfamily trustees play an integral role in determining grant-making policies.
3. *Trusts*: A foundation or fund in which the responsibility for operations has passed into the hands of friends, partners, or

business associates of the original donor is often called a trust. In many cases, trusts are administered by law firms or banks.

4. *Professional foundations*: This category consists of foundations, such as the Ford Foundation, in which control of assets and activities has passed entirely into the hands of a nonfamily board of trustees, which defines policies and programs that are administered by a professional staff.

5. *Community foundations*: This type of foundation is established in a specific community with funds derived from a variety of individuals, rather than from one individual, and is governed by a board of community representatives. There is usually only one community foundation serving a particular area. Community foundations, such as the New York Community Trust, the San Francisco Foundation, and the Cleveland Foundation, respond to the special concerns and interests of the people in their communities. Individuals who contribute to the community foundation have the option of restricting the types of gifts made from their funds or allowing the staff and board of the foundation to make all grant-making decisions. Often, many of the grants made by community foundations result from the wishes of the foundation's donors rather than from decisions by its board of trustees.

   Today, community foundations are the fastest-growing type of foundation. Many community foundations have professional full-time staff to publish information on foundation activities, to meet with prospective grantees, and to carry out carefully planned contribution programs.

6. *Corporate foundations*: This type of foundation is established by a corporation to maintain a regular philanthropic program (see Chapter 4). The giving policies of a corporate foundation are usually consistent with the goals and interests of the corporation. Not all corporations have a corporate foundation but may instead make donations through corporate contribution programs. However, some corporations operate both a corporate foundation and a corporate giving program.

It is important to be aware of the term *operating foundation*. An operating foundation is a not-for-profit organization that uses its endowed funds for its own programs. It is not a grant-making entity.

Most foundations are managed by a board of directors made up of the donor and the donor's family members, friends, or colleagues. These individuals usually serve in a voluntary capacity. The vast majority of foundations do not employ a staff, hold regular office hours, or publish information describing their activities.

Usually only the larger community, corporate, and professional foundations employ a full-time staff and operate under well-developed grant-making guidelines. Staff members thoroughly investigate project areas and carefully screen applications. Professionally staffed foundations are equipped to handle requests for information and deal with the public.

## WHAT DETERMINES A FOUNDATION'S GIVING POLICY?

A foundation's giving policy is designed to provide either general purpose funds or funds for a clearly defined program. A foundation with a giving policy of providing general purpose funds usually offers grants to a wide range of organizations or individuals in the fields of health, education, social welfare, and culture. The giving policy of a particular foundation will often reflect the interests of the foundation's original donor, the donor's family, or the foundation's board of trustees. Many foundations determine how they will distribute funds by identifying problems in a particular discipline. The needs of the local community or problems of national or international concern may also affect a foundation's giving policies. Awards are granted to institutions that have projects designed to solve those problems. For example, a foundation may be interested in U.S. relations with the People's Republic of China. An arts organization's plan to present a major ballet company from China may be of special interest to such a foundation.

Some foundations are endowed for a special purpose and support only programs related to that purpose. Professional foundations, in particular, will limit their grants to a few specific program areas that are perceived as important to society. As social conditions change, these foundations will adjust the focus of their giving programs accordingly.

## WHAT KIND OF SUPPORT IS AVAILABLE?

In addition to general purpose and special project grants, certain foundations make grants for capital projects and endowments. Foundations are usually more willing than businesses to consider providing seed money for experimental projects, and foundations do not usually require the same kind of public relations benefits from their grant-making activities as businesses desire.

Foundation grants may be annual or multi-year, depending on the policies of the foundation. Small foundations are more apt to give annual support, whereas large foundations often prefer to fund special projects over several years. Furthermore, some foundations will discontinue support to an organization after two or three years of involvement. Foundations with giving polices that are designed to solve problems will want to focus on new projects and areas of interest when the problem has been or is near to being solved. Many foundations also have a dollar limitation on grants awarded to a single organization in a given year.

## HOW TO APPROACH FOUNDATIONS FOR SUPPORT

Many of the larger foundations include in their annual reports or publish separately information on funding policies, areas of interest, and application requirements. It is important to review these guidelines carefully so that the grant proposal addresses areas of concern to the foundation. In cases where no publications are available, information can be gleaned from entries in a number of reference books on foundations and research profiles compiled along the lines described in Chapter 3.

Proposals to foundations that are concerned with addressing specific problems can often be detailed and lengthy (see "Foundation Special Project Proposal" in Appendix I). Proposals of this type are best written using a problem-solving approach in which the organization describes how its project will meet needs or solve problems already defined as areas of special interest to the foundation.

As in all areas of fundraising, personal contact with foundation trustees and staff is enormously helpful in the grant-seeking process.

## HOW FOUNDATIONS MAKE FUNDING DECISIONS

Funding decisions are typically made by the foundation's board of trustees after a presentation by the staff or by a board member if there is no staff. The board meets periodically during the year to make its funding decisions.

Prior to each meeting, the foundation staff or designated board member examines the proposals received to find the most interesting and appropriate projects to bring to the board's attention. A short summary of the project is prepared. It is this document, in most cases, rather than the original proposal, that is initially reviewed by the board. Since the staff member or designated board member is the key person in determining which proposals the board will see, it is extremely important to develop a good working relationship with this individual.

When the foundation board meets, the first part of the meeting is usually devoted to a discussion of the foundation's investments and other business matters. During the second part of the meeting, grant proposals are presented and discussed.

The foundation board is most often concerned with the following questions when reviewing proposals:

- Does the project address foundation program areas creatively?
- Is the organization qualified to implement the project?

- Does the organization have a solid reputation in its field?
- Is the organization's board of trustees capable of providing leadership?
- How long will the organization require support from the foundation?
- Will the project be self-supporting, or will it develop other means of grant support after a reasonable amount of time?

Following this inquiry, the foundation's board will make its funding decisions. Award letters are then sent to the successful applicants; in most cases, letters are also sent to those organizations not awarded funds.

Once the organization has received a foundation grant, it is important to keep the foundation formally apprised of the progress of the project by submitting progress reports. These serve to update the foundation on the status of the project and to highlight major new developments. Reports should be accompanied by appropriate budgets and selected supplementary materials. Often foundations will request interim and final reports from the organization. These reports must be as well prepared as the original proposal. The best way to build a continuing relationship with a foundation is to manage the project successfully, keeping the foundation informed throughout the process.

# Chapter 6
# Individuals

Individuals are by far the most significant source of support for America's not-for-profit organizations. In 1986 individuals contributed $71.72 billion—82.2 percent of all philanthropic support. This compares with $4.50 billion donated by corporations and $5.17 billion by foundations.

Americans contributed $40.90 billion to religious causes in 1986. According to the American Association of Fund Raising Counsel, Inc., this represents nearly half of the total funds contributed to philanthropic causes in the United States. Hospitals and health-related causes received $12.26 billion; education, $12.73 billion; social services, $9.13 billion; arts and humanities, $5.83 billion; civic activities, $2.38 billion; and other causes, $3.99 billion.

Arts and cultural organizations receive the support of individuals who enjoy and believe in the organizations' activities and feel a certain satisfaction in contributing to the betterment of the community. It can be prestigious and exciting to be a patron of a cultural organization. Tax incentives, special privileges and premiums, peer pressure, and personal ambitions are other reasons for contributing. Current tax law allows an individual to take deductions of up to 50 percent of adjusted gross income for cash contributions made to organizations carrying 501(c)(3) status (nonprivate foundations). Support from individuals is usually solicited through personal contact or through direct-mail appeals.

## PATRONS

Patrons are those individuals who make large donations to an organization. The minimum contribution designating patron level will vary from organization to organization Many patrons make donations annually. Patrons are extremely important to an organization because their gifts are, in most cases, a reliable source of unrestricted funds that can be used to support innovative projects that a foundation or corporation may consider too risky. Most important, patrons have a substantial interest in the organizations they support and can provide access to other individuals who may also become patrons of the organization.

Unlike funding agencies, individuals are not regulated by giving policies, timeframes, and decision-making committees. Patrons can give as much as they wish to whomever they wish; because there are few bureaucratic strings attached to these kinds of gifts, patron support is very desirable to an organization.

On the other hand, patron support can create different problems. An individual making a major grant may wish to be involved in making programmatic decisions. This can compromise the mission of the organization. An important patron who is also a board member may exert too much influence over members, inhibiting the board's governing process. Patrons may also develop allegiances to new organizations without prior warning, leaving the discarded organization in serious financial difficulty.

Large organizations, such as major museums, civic ballets, symphony orchestras, and opera companies, offer glamour and prestige to their supporters and therefore attract the greatest number of patrons who contribute the largest amounts of funds.

Smaller organizations can also generate support from individuals. Patrons often feel more important when they play a major role in the very survival of a small organization than when they are one of hundreds of supporters of a large one. A group working in an experimental style, for example, will often be too controversial to receive funds from businesses or foundations. Patron support can be the primary source of funds for this kind of organization.

Organizations with fairly "conservative" programs may attract many of their patrons from the professional community—lawyers, doctors, and corporate executives. These patrons are usually very reliable and will contribute annually for many years; and because many of them know one another, they can easily introduce their friends and colleagues to the work of the organization.

In order to attract patron support, the development director must understand the following:

- How to identify prospective patrons
- How to approach patrons for support
- How to sustain a patron's interest in the organization

## How to Identify Prospective Patrons

Patrons are often well-known figures in the community, and their participation in the activities of the organization can bring it considerable credibility and public awareness. The best way to identify these prospective patrons is through other patrons. A party held by a supporter to introduce friends and colleagues to the director of the organization can be invaluable as a means of developing a prospect list.

Board members can also be helpful by identifying and recruiting individuals whom they know. Often board members themselves will be patrons, with networks of friends whom they will bring to opening nights and special events. All board members should be encouraged to recruit their friends and colleagues.

The development director should also investigate responses to direct-mail appeals. If, for example, a $250 gift comes in as a result of a direct-mail appeal, the prospective patron should be researched in *The Directory of Directors, Who's Who,* and other appropriate reference books to determine his or her occupation, place of business, and social standing. Since the initial donation has already been sent to the organization, interest is confirmed; the best method must then be determined for developing a relationship with that individual.

Collecting membership lists from the leading social organizations and service organizations in the community is also a good idea. Potential patrons may be found in the memberships of various civic clubs, such as the Junior League and the League of Women Voters. Often the same name will show up on a variety of different lists. The kinds of organizations an individual supports will indicate the individual's particular interests. For example, if a name appears on the donor lists of four major museums and not on the list of any performing arts organizations, it may be that the individual is exclusively interested in visual arts, and more research should be done to determine if the individual is a likely prospect for a performing arts organization.

Directories such as *Who's Who* can be used not only to identify patrons but also to find out more about them. It is also very helpful to gain information about the prospective patron's family by reading the local newspapers' society columns and obituaries as well as notices announcing engagements, weddings, and births. The *Reverse Telephone Directory,* which is indexed by addresses in a specific locality rather than by last names, is helpful in identifying persons residing in a particular neighborhood.

## How to Approach Patrons for Support

Approaching patrons for support requires discretion and an understanding of each patron's likes and dislikes. One patron may prefer simply to send a check to the organization every year, while another will request a written proposal. Some patrons expect an annual lunch with the artistic director or program head and like to be brought up-to-date personally on all aspects of the organization's activities before agreeing to make their annual contributions. A few patrons like to make their gifts public and will present a check to the organization at a board meeting.

Historically, patrons have had their largess demonstrated by having a building, theater, rehearsal room, study center, cafeteria, or garden named in honor of themselves or a loved one. Naming opportunities are one of the most effective ways to generate major gifts and to provide recognition in perpetuity to the donor. On a smaller scale, naming seats in a theater (see Appendix I, "Seat Endowment Brochure"), trees in a garden, or scholarships for students after patrons is a good fundraising strategy.

There is simply no system available for soliciting patrons except to work with them in the manner they prefer. They should be made to feel comfortable and rewarded in return for their generosity. Usually the program or artistic director has a close relationship with patrons, particularly those who have been involved with the organization for any length of time. When such a relationship exists, this individual is the key participant in the actual solicitation, and the development director helps with the follow-up and prepares written requests.

## How to Sustain a Patron's Interest in the Organization

Patrons should receive personal thank you notes after they have made their contributions and should be kept well informed about the organization's activities throughout the year. They should be placed on the organization's mailing lists and invited to the most prestigious events.

As major donors, patrons should be sent special items in the mail, such as copies of good reviews, ideas for future productions or exhibits, and advance notices of open rehearsals and special events. Patrons' interest in the organization will be sustained by reinforcing a sense of shared ownership in the organization. Patrons are sought after by many organizations and therefore must be treated in a manner that will maintain their interest and not become an annoyance.

## LOWER LEVEL CONTRIBUTORS

The solicitation of lower level contributors is often done through direct-mail or telefundraising appeals. Simply stated, a direct-mail appeal is a fundraising technique whereby the organization requests support from individuals by mailing them a package of materials designed to introduce them to the organization and interest them enough to make a contribution. (See Appendix I, "Direct-Mail Package I" and "Direct-Mail Package II," for examples of direct-mail appeals.) A telefundraising appeal is very similar to the direct-mail technique, except that the organization uses telephone callers to request support. This is often a more costly technique than direct mail, but more effective.

Many cultural organizations have a membership organization to which an individual contributes and thereby is entitled to receive benefits based on the size of the contributions. Small gift fundraising not only gives the organization additional income but also helps uncover potential new board members, volunteers, and patrons; it also increases public awareness of the organization.

## Direct Mail

This discussion will focus on direct-mail fundraising appeals that involve mailing to at least 10,000 households. Large- and medium-sized organizations will generally use direct mail as a part of their overall fundraising campaign. Sometimes, a small organization that has a broad-based constituency can successfully generate funds through direct mail. Because of the high start-up costs required to launch a direct-mail campaign, an organization should seriously consider the financial risk involved before making the investment. Executing a direct-mail campaign involves the following procedures:

- Scheduling and budgeting
- Assembling the production team
- Selecting the mailing lists
- Producing the direct-mail package
- Following up with donors who have not renewed
- Recording donor information

### Scheduling and Budgeting

There are two types of direct-mail campaigns: prospect or acquisition mailings, which are designed to acquire new donors; and renewal mailings, which are intended to solicit donations from current donors. Before undertaking an acquisition mailing, the institution must decide if there is a sufficient number of potential new prospects to warrant the time and expense required to implement a direct-mail fundraising campaign.

The cost of acquiring the mailing lists, designing and printing the direct-mail package, hiring the lettershop to fold and insert materials and to attach labels, and buying postage can be considerable, but it can pay off in the long run if carefully budgeted and administered. A comprehensive budget should therefore be developed prior to initiating the campaign.

The organization's initial investment in an acquisition mailing will rarely be recouped after the first mailing. It will, however, repay itself many times over through renewals. Statistics indicate that a significant percentage of new donors will renew their contributions—at a much lower solicitation cost—and that many will continue to give for five years or longer. In addition, these donors could potentially be solicited two or three times during the season. However, these subsequent solicitations should request support for a special project or theme as opposed to the annual request for general support.

The organization should plan its entire direct-mail campaign well in advance of the season, taking into account other organizational activities that may conflict, such as special events and subscription mailings. Direct-mail campaigns undertaken during the holiday season or the summer months are typically the least effective.

Once the mailing date is determined, use a reverse timetable to set deadlines for acquiring mailing lists and for designing, printing, and assembling the package—usually two to three months of preparation are required before the actual mail date.

A carefully planned campaign will allow enough time to raise funds to implement the plan, to determine the projected cash flow based on realistic projections, to hire personnel, and to carry out the plan.

## Assembling the Production Team

The development director must assemble a qualified group of people to execute the direct-mail campaign. The production team should include a list broker, who is responsible for assembling the lists; a copywriter; a graphic designer; a printer; and lettershop personnel, who assemble, label, and mail the package. The development director should thoroughly investigate each potential member of the team by examining samples of their work, inspecting their work facilities, and evaluating the responses from their references.

A good list broker will develop a complete understanding of donor response in the past and the results of other direct-mail campaigns before recommending which lists should be purchased. The list broker should also be thoroughly informed about these lists, knowing the number of names on each list, its origin and effectiveness, and its purchase price. In addition, the list broker should know which other organizations have used the lists, and how often.

It is important that the copywriter—whether a staff member or a professional direct-mail copywriter from outside the organization—be able to convey the uniqueness of the organization. If a staff member is going to write the copy, that individual should not only be a good writer but should also have a thorough understanding of direct-mail fundraising and the ability to write the kind of copy that motivates people to contribute.

The graphic designer should have good design and graphic skills and the ability to supervise the package through its production phase. The actual design must complement the copy and not overshadow it.

It is important to find a printer who produces high-quality work at a reasonable price and delivers on time. If possible, the organization should develop an ongoing relationship with one or two good printers who are trustworthy and reliable.

The lettershop must be aware of all current postal regulations and procedures for handling bulk mail. The lettershop must be reliable, affordable, and efficient. An effective production team is extremely important to the success of a direct-mail effort.

### Selecting Mailing Lists

Before a direct-mail package can be created, it must be decided to whom the mailing will be sent. There are four different target groups from which an arts or cultural organization can develop its mailing lists:

1. *Current donors*: These are donors who have made a donation to the organization within the past 24 months. This is the "hottest" list because these individuals have a proven interest in the organization. The individuals on this list should receive personalized renewal mailings. These individuals are also the prime candidates to receive additional mail solicitations throughout the year for special projects. Statistics indicate that one-third of the individuals on a list of current donors will make multiple contributions.

2. *Subscribers, frequent attendees, and other known participants*: These persons have demonstrated their interest in the institution but have not yet become donors. Lists of such people are considered "warm" lists, and solicitations should be sent to encourage these individuals to extend their support by making a contribution.

3. *Inactive former donors*: Past donors who have not contributed during the last 24 months are in this category. Usually direct-mail solicitations should not be sent to inactive donors more than twice a year. However, this group may be sent a special "why-have-you-forsaken-us" appeal that asks the recipient why they have stopped supporting the organization.

4. *New prospects*: There are a variety of "cold" prospect lists that can be used to contact new prospective donors. These lists are called acquisition lists or new prospect lists. They include donor lists from similar organizations; common-denominator lists, which include individuals in a particular occupation, zip-code area, or income bracket; lists of persons who buy through mail order catalogues, such as book club members; magazine subscriber lists; and lists that can be obtained from a list broker. A major source of information regarding mailing lists is the *Direct Mail List Rates and Data Directory*, published by Standard Rate and Data Service.

When mailing to any acquisition list, be sure to review the names carefully so that no current donors are sent requests for support. Exchanging lists with other organizations in order to avoid having to purchase lists may be a good idea; however, many organizations have policies prohibiting the sale or exchange of their lists.

Direct-mail lists can be tested by mailing sample request packages to a small number of names on each list to find out the lists that are the most effective. This type of testing helps the organization select the lists it will use in a campaign. Testing can be a valuable means of learning about the response rate of potential contributors, but it is important to use a statistically valid test base in order to predict results accurately. Someone knowledgeable about testing, such as a direct-mail consultant, can help determine what numerical base is required to produce an accurate sample response.

## Producing the Direct-Mail Package

Producing the direct-mail package involves the following steps:

- Choosing the components and theme
- Writing the copy
- Designing and producing the artwork
- Printing, assembling, and mailing

### *Choosing the Components and Theme*

Once the lists have been selected, the development director must determine the components of the direct-mail package. These usually include an outside or carrier envelope; an appeal letter; a reply device of some kind; and a reply envelope. In addition, a brochure or gift card listing premiums offered at various contribution levels may be part of the package.

Developing the format, however, means more than simply deciding what pieces will be included. It also means selecting a design concept that will communicate the message of the organization in the most effective and least expensive way. It is not necessary to spend a great deal of money on custom-made envelopes and paper, or on extravagant color designs. It is hard to convey the organization's need for funds in a package that looks as though it cost a great deal to produce. A simple straightforward format that is easy to read and gets to the point usually produces the best results.

### *Writing the Copy*

The appeal letter is the most important element in the direct-mail package because it is through the letter that the initial contact is made with the prospective donor. Letters can be personalized, or a generic salutation, such as "Dear Friend," can be used. A large-scale mailing that is personalized will require computerization.

The writer for the campaign must determine the type of appeal that will motivate each particular group of readers to contribute. For example, if an appeal is being made to the community in which the organization is located, then the letter may stress the civic role played by the organization. Appeal letters may also mention concrete results accomplished with contributions of various amounts. For example, an organization can indicate that a contribution of a certain amount will be used to purchase a new orchestra stand or provide one full scholarship.

The appeal letter serves a different purpose in a mailing to renewal candidates. A renewal letter is personalized and tends to be shorter than a letter to potential new donors. Because the recipients are already familiar with the organization, the renewal letter should reinforce their role in the work of the organization rather than introduce the organization to them. For example, the appeal letter may say to prospective new donors, "You may not know it but the XYZ Theater is the only cultural organization in Illinois committed exclusively to creating new American plays." On the other hand, the appeal letter to renewal candidates may read, "Through your help, the XYZ Theater has continued to thrive as the only cultural organization in Illinois committed exclusively to creating new American plays."

There are a variety of letter-writing techniques that can influence the success of a direct-mail campaign. The word *you*, for example, is the most important word in an appeal letter: "You can play an important role in the future of a great American dance company." Using *you*, personalizes the reader's importance to the work of the organization and imparts a greater motivation to contribute. *You* should always be used instead of *we* in a solicitation letter because more responsibility is given to the reader. Other stylistic devices, such as italicizing or underlining passages or printing certain paragraphs or sentences in a different color, emphasize key ideas in a fundraising letter. However, it is important not to go too far in employing extravagant printing techniques to make a point. For example, letters using four colors or an unusual format tend to end up looking depersonalized—and expensive. It is difficult for readers to relate to them.

Once acquainted with the overall theme of the letter, the reader must be convinced that the programmatic purpose of the organization and its importance to the community merits support. Throughout the appeal the reader should be treated as a participant, or should be invited to participate, in the work of the organization. Try to instill a sense of ownership in the reader. The institution may wish to select someone to sign the letter who personifies the theme of the mailing. Often this will be the organization's director or board chair, but it could also be a well-known artist, community leader, or beneficiary of the institution's funds. If possible, request a specific amount of money and indicate what premiums will be given in return for a contribution.

Premiums can be extremely simple or very elaborate, depending on the organization. The most important thing is to be creative and offer the most imaginative and attractive premiums as possible. Use premiums to strengthen the organization's relationship to its donors. For example, attending an open rehearsal can make donors feel that they have had an opportunity to see something special and out of the ordinary. Donors carrying tote bags bearing the organization's name and logo help to give the organization greater visibility in the community.

The value and quality of donor premiums usually increase with the amount of the donation. At the lower contribution level, premiums often include free subscriptions to donor newsletters and discounts on all other items offered as premiums. At the next contribution level, donors receive all the items offered to those contributors at lower levels, plus such benefits as tote bags, T-shirts, records, passes to open rehearsals, and priority seating. The largest donations warrant special VIP premiums, such as free parking passes, priority seating, books and posters signed by the organization's artists, complimentary drinks in the patrons' lounge, invitations to opening night parties, and dinners with the director, board members, or visiting artists and dignitaries.

A renewal letter must include a mention of the donor's last gift. Be sure to thank the donor again for his or her support; indicate how the donor has helped, and build a solid case for his or her continued assistance. Conclude a renewal letter by thanking the donor for the contribution he or she is about to send.

It is appropriate in an annual renewal letter to ask donors to think about increasing their annual contribution. The amount of the suggested increase should be mentioned in the letter. Special premiums can be offered as an incentive to the donor to make a larger donation. Increased contributions from existing donors are a major objective in the success of a direct-mail effort to solicit renewals.

Many different kinds of reply devices are currently used in direct-mail packages. It is very important that the device selected be simple. The organization wants to make it as easy as possible for the reader to respond. The reply device should briefly summarize the theme of the letter—"Yes, I want to support new American plays!" It should also explain what gifts of various amounts will enable the organization to accomplish; mention the premiums available for contribution of specific amounts; provide instructions for making out the check; indicate the portion of the contribution that is tax deductible; and thank the donor again for joining the organization's family of contributors. A reply device can be part of the reply envelope or it can be a separate insert. It is sometimes a good idea to have the reply device attached to the reply envelope so that the potential donor can easily mail it back to the organization. Briefly restating the theme on the reply envelope can provide additional motivation for contributing.

The reply envelope is merely an envelope large enough to hold a check and the reply device. The address of the organization should be clearly printed on the front of the envelope. The question of whether to pay for return postage or not will have to be decided by the organization. If funds are available, it is a recommended procedure to use a postage-paid business reply envelope, or BRE, because this makes it easier for the donor to respond. Postage is paid to the post office only for those envelopes that are returned to the organization.

The reply devices and/or reply envelopes for new donors should be coded to indicate from which list the donors have been taken so that the organization can determine the lists that have elicited the best response.

Coding, a system of alphabetical, numerical, or color identification, is used to distinguish responses from various lists, zip code areas, or occupational groups. There are many ways to code direct-mail appeals. The development director should select the most efficient coding system for a particular direct-mail campaign by observing how other organizations code or by seeking advice from a member of the production team or a professional direct-mail consultant.

Renewal solicitations should also be coded in order to learn which techniques most successfully prompted donors to renew: a first request for renewal, a reminder letter, or a follow-up telephone call. For example, donors are mailed first renewal notices, which include reply cards coded with the letter $A$. Few donors respond. Nonresponsive donors are sent second notices, including a reply card coded with the letter $B$. Again, few respond. Finally, remaining nonresponsive donors are telephoned and solicited for a gift. A significant number agree and are sent response forms coded with a $C$, which are subsequently returned with the donors' checks. At the end of the campaign, a response analysis can be done to determine which technique produced the best results. If $C$ generated a large number of responses—as it did in this example—it suggests that a telephone appeal is an important component in the renewal campaign.

The carrier envelope is usually a standard-sized envelope on which an address label is affixed, or one with a window through which the address appears. The return address of the institution should also be printed on the envelope so recipients will know who is writing to them.

In addition to the appeal letter, there are a number of other enclosures, such as a brochure, that can be included in the package to enhance the written copy. To determine the copy components and format of a direct-mail package, it is often helpful to examine different kinds of packages from a variety of organizations. Each piece of the package should be drafted and revised until a clear and convincing message is created.

It may be easier to begin writing copy by drafting the simpler pieces of the package first, saving the appeal letter for last. Once the copy has been written, it should be examined by the development director to be sure that the information is accurate and that the style is appropriate.

Sometimes it is a good idea to test different copy approaches to determine which elicits the best results. Other variables, such as the use of window envelopes versus labels, or the use of a postage-paid business reply envelope versus one that requires postage stamps, are among the many aspects of the direct-mail package that can be tested. The coding used for a response device could be similar to that used for a renewal appeal. Make sure only one variable is tested at a time.

## *Designing and Producing the Artwork*

A graphic artist should be enlisted to design a package that enhances the message stated in the copy. An imaginative design concept will be the most successful; but it is important not to let the design dominate the package. The designer, whose work should be supervised by the development director, must be aware that the weight and size of the package affect the costs of producing and mailing it.

Once the senior staff of the organization has approved the components, format, copy, and design of the package, production can begin. It is the artist's responsibility to make sure that the layout, paste-up, and typesetting of each piece of the package are done properly. Several individuals should proofread the final copy before it goes to the printer.

## *Printing, Assembling, and Mailing*

Once the package has been adequately proofed, it is ready for printing. Make sure to have written estimates from the printer before running the job. Also, ask to see a blueprint of the package to confirm everything one last time before it goes to press.

The lettershop should be informed in advance as to when the materials will be delivered by the printer so that schedules can be arranged accordingly. If address labels are being used, it is a good idea to print the carrier envelopes first and have them delivered to the lettershop so that the labels can be affixed while the rest of the package is being printed. If window envelopes are being used, there is no need to print these first because the mailing addresses will be printed on the actual letter.

Before the lettershop assembles the package for mailing, a sample should be put together and approved by the organization to make sure each component is folded correctly and placed in the envelopes properly. Once the packages have been assembled and sealed, they must be sorted according to postal regulations.

The development director should be aware of the various mailing options available and should consider cost and delivery time in determining the best mailing procedure. Organizations that have established or wish to establish ongoing direct-mail campaigns should obtain the most up-to-date pamphlets from the postal service that explain the requirements of first-class, third-class, and fourth-class bulk mailings. Organizations can also subscribe to the *Domestic Mail Manual*, which is the foremost source of postal regulations, and the *Postal Bulletin*, which lists all changes in regulations that have not yet been incorporated into the *Domestic Mail Manual*. All of the above sources are available through local post offices.

Most not-for-profit organizations mail first-class or third-class, also referred to as "bulk mail," depending on the size and nature of the mailing. Renewal solicitations, for example, and all personal correspondence are mailed first-class. First-class mail requires no sorting and can be dropped either at the post office or in any mail box. This option is the most expensive, but the delivery time is usually only one or two days, depending on the efficiency of the mail service within a particular geographic area.

Other first-class mail options include presort first-class mail and carrier-route presort first-class mail, both of which are less expensive than regular first-class but require sorting according to specific regulations. An organization that mails at least 500 pieces can use either first-class presort option.

Many nonprofit organizations use business reply envelopes (BREs), which allow patrons to respond to an appeal without paying postage. In order to use BREs, the organization pays an annual fee to the post office and maintains an account there that is depleted as the returned mail comes in. In this way, the institution pays only for what is returned. If BREs are to be used, the envelope must conform to post office requirements.

Cultural organizations often send acquisition and subscription campaign mailings, as well as promotions for single-ticket sales, newsletters, and calendars of events, at third-class bulk rates. Third-class mail is generally used when trying to reach a large audience and when a personalized look is not the most essential element in communicating to the reader.

In order to take advantage of the special not-for-profit third-class bulk rate, an organization must apply and meet the qualifications outlined by postal regulations. The not-for-profit bulk mail permit must be renewed annually by the organization. Third-class bulk rates apply to any mailing of 200 or more pieces sorted according to zip code and bundled as specified by postal regulations. Third-class bulk mail generally takes ten days to three weeks for delivery.

There are also different mailing options within the third-class category, including third-class carrier-route presort rates and five-digit presort rates, which offer organizations opportunities for even greater discounts. Again, regulations concerning sorting, bundling, and labeling should be thoroughly investigated prior to mailing.

The lettershop should complete its work in time for the organization to meet its targeted mail date. Timing is important to a mailing, and a few weeks of delay can seriously affect campaign results. Refer to Chart 6.1, the direct-mail copy and package checklist, for a handy review of the most important points to keep in mind in conducting a direct-mail campaign.

## CHART 6.1 DIRECT-MAIL COPY AND PACKAGE CHECKLIST

☐ Does your copy tell the story clearly, dramatically, and persuasively? Do you have a story to tell?

☐ Have you captured your prospect in the lead?

☐ Is your letter personal enough? Write "you" copy, not "we" copy. Remember, using typeset copy will detract from a personal look.

☐ Have you determined the right audience for your appeal through tests of lists to different constituencies?

☐ Have you established a donor profile for your own house list?

☐ Have you taken the time to explain what your organization is and what it does? Give a little background in the letter and brochure.

☐ Have you been specific enough about what the donor's contribution will do?

☐ Are the suggested gift amounts high enough? Remember that if all you ask for is a dollar, that's probably all you'll get. Ask for $25 and $50, $100 and $1,000.

☐ Have you remembered to ask for contributions more than once in the body of the letter and again in the brochure and on the response device?

☐ Have you spelled out the action you want the reader to take?

☐ Is your signer someone people care about, respect, or identify with?

☐ Have you done the homework necessary—such as visiting program sites, talking to program directors, and reading the letters from program beneficiaries—to write an appeal that is timely and filled with hard facts and human interest?

☐ Have you striven for the right word when writing your appeals? Mark Twain said, "The difference between the right word and the almost right word is the difference between lightning and a lightning bug."

☐ Have you looked at your mailing pieces carefully? Do they look too expensive? Are they bland? Do they have the right graphic impact?

☐ Have you tested enough new approaches in copy, layout, and lists? Remember to test one, and only one, thing at a time.

☐ Have you experimented with teaser copy on the carrier envelope and/or in the letter?

☐ Have you thought to use a P.S. at the bottom or top of the page for special emphasis?

☐ Have you thought to use a second color for emphasis on the letterhead, signature, or within the body of the appeal letter?

☐ Has your copy been approved by the signer and the powers that be? Have you allowed enough time in your planning for this process?

☐ Have you tested one-page letters against two-, three-, and four-page letters?

☐ Have you enclosed a response device that makes it easy for the donor to respond? Have you remembered to suggest gift amounts on the response device?

☐ Have you tested a postage-paid business reply envelope versus a reply envelope to which the donor will have to affix a stamp?

☐ Have you tested a package with and without a brochure?

☐ Have you tested generic letters versus computer-generated personalized letters for prospect mailings?

☐ Have you tested a computer gift-form for renewals?

## CHART 6.1  DIRECT-MAIL COPY AND PACKAGE CHECKLIST (continued)

☐ Have you tested the various nonprofit or first-class postage possibilities, such as imprinting an indicia, using a postage meter, or affixing embossed or precancelled stamps?

☐ Have you remembered to key all your BREs or mailing labels so that tests can be properly analyzed?

☐ Have you remembered to confine your tests to only one variable at a time?

☐ Do you have a well-thought-out renewal strategy and not just a once-a-year appeal? Remember, it will probably take four to six appeals a year to maintain a healthy renewal rate.

☐ Have you segmented your list of renewal candidates by gift size and by the date of the most recent gift so that you make the most cost-effective appeals?

☐ Do you try to upgrade donor gifts by conducting at least one or two renewal appeals a year?

☐ Have you thought to suggest a specific gift amount in these appeals to upgrade contributions?

☐ Have you asked for more than one gift a year from your donors? At least a third will make multiple gifts if properly approached.

☐ Have you researched large gifts for potentially higher support?

☐ Have you reported to donors on what their previous gifts have accomplished? Remember, people are more interested in helping people than institutions.

☐ Have you remembered to give donors due credit for being supporters, personalizing the appeal to them as much as possible?

☐ Have you specified benefits to members, subscribers, and donors in appeals to both renewal candidates and new prospects?

☐ Have you thought to ask for monthly pledges from your donors?

☐ Have you thought to ask donors for referral names?

☐ Have you ever suggested to your donors that they leave a bequest to your institution?

☐ Have you acknowledged gifts above a certain amount with a receipt and letter?

☐ Have you answered genuine complaints?

☐ Have you tried to reactivate lapsed donors with special personalized appeals?

☐ For planning appeals, do you use a reverse timetable?

☐ Have you remembered to check with the post office to review mailing options for sorting and stamping?

☐ Have you gotten competitive bids on all printing and lettershop work?

☐ Have you remembered to send a sample package to the lettershop? Are you sure all the elements are machine insertable? Do they fit into the carrier envelope? Do they conform to postal regulations?

☐ Have you always provided clear written instructions to the printer and the lettershop, specifying color and paper stock?

☐ Have you worked out your package costs before moving ahead with a mailing?

☐ Have you remembered to order a full year's or season's supply of standard supplies at once rather than one mailing at a time?

## CHART 6.1  DIRECT-MAIL COPY AND PACKAGE CHECKLIST (continued)

☐ Have you mailed a package to yourself and your colleagues in different zip codes to determine if and when the packages are received?

☐ Have you mailed on your predetermined mail date?

☐ Have you remembered to oversee suppliers and the lettershop to ensure that mailings go out when they are scheduled?

☐ Have you set up systems to record gifts and to analyze returns?

☐ Have you tracked list results carefully by the date mailed, the number of packages mailed to each list, the number of positive responses received from each list, the amount of income generated from each list, the percentage of gifts received, the average-size gift, and the amount of income generated per 1,000 pieces mailed?

☐ Have you thought to trade your own donor list for another donor list? Compare results achieved using rented lists versus traded lists and you will discover why so many institutions trade lists.

☐ Do you have reasonable expectations for the return from a mailing to new prospects? Breaking even or a little better is all most mailers can expect from cold prospects.

☐ Have you borrowed a good idea when you have seen one? Start reading all that mail you get and see what is effective and how you can improve upon it in your own mailings.

The Direct-Mail Copy and Package Checklist was developed by Charlene Divoky and Associates; Sanky Perlowin Associates; and Roger Craver, president, Craver Mathews Smith and Company. Permission to print the checklist in this book is granted by the aforementioned organizations.

### Following Up with Donors Who Have Not Renewed

If a donor does not respond to the renewal solicitation sent on the anniversary of the last gift, the organization should send another letter of request one month later. If that letter produces no results, a third appeal should be sent, gently stressing the fact that the gift has not been renewed. If there is still no response, a telephone call is in order. As stated earlier, the renewal solicitations should be coded to help evaluate which letter or technique most successfully prompted donors to renew.

Some organizations will conduct a phonathon every four to six months, calling recalcitrant donors to find out why they have not renewed and if they would like to do so. Special phonathons for inactive donors—those who have not contributed in 24 months—have a 10 to 12 percent recovery rate and should be held at least once a year. (A complete discussion of larger-scale telefundraising campaigns appears after this section on direct mail.)

**Recording Donor Information**

As responses begin to come in from an acquisition mailing, it is important to establish a good system for recording information about the campaign and about individual donors. The important aspects of each direct-mail campaign should be recorded and kept on file, including information regarding budgets, plans, correspondence, schedules, contracts, and agreements. Information on the performance of each list used in the campaign should be charted, showing the number of packages mailed to each list, the date the packages were mailed, the number of positive responses received from each list, the amount of income generated from each list, the percentage of gifts received, the average amount of an individual gift, and the amount of income generated per thousand pieces mailed.

Each column on the direct-mail results report (see Chart 6.2) should be tabulated weekly. Final results should be computed at the conclusion of the campaign, about 60 days after the mail date. The subtotals will reveal information about the performance of each list, and the final total will indicate the gross return from all the lists. The expenses of the campaign should be deducted from the gross income to reveal the net income. In addition, the total number of responses should be compared to the total number of packages mailed to determine the percentage of return, or response rate, for the entire campaign.

It is also important to compile accurate results from the renewal campaign that indicate the percentage of donors who renewed and at what level, the number of donors who increased their donations, and how may donors became inactive.

Reliable information on each individual donor should be recorded on an alphabetical file card or in a computer file. This information should include the following:

- Name of donor
- Address
- Date and amount of gift
- Purpose of gift
- Contribution history over the previous five years
- Additional relevant information, such as business

If records are kept manually as opposed to on computer, a separate chronological card file should be maintained that duplicates information contained in the alphabetical file but that organizes donor cards by the month in which a gift was received. The organization can then solicit renewals six months or a year after the first gift arrives without having to scan all of the alphabetical cards. affiliation or special funding interests

## CHART 6.2 DIRECT-MAIL RESULTS REPORT

| Computer Code Number | List Name | Date Mailed | Number of Packages Mailed | Number of Positive Responses Received | Amount of Income Generated | Percentage Received* | Average Gift** | Dollars Received per Thousand*** |
|---|---|---|---|---|---|---|---|---|
| | | | | | | | | |

\* Percentage Received is the number of positive responses received, divided by the number of packages mailed.
\*\* Average Gift is the amount of income generated, divided by the number of positive responses received.
\*\*\* Dollars Received per Thousand is the amount of income generated, divided by the number of packages mailed, multiplied by 1,000.

It is vital to maintain mailing lists that are current, accurate, and usable at all times. Accurate lists keep postage costs down and help the organization avoid the mistake of mailing a solicitation to the old address of someone who has moved. Donor lists should be updated and corrected on an ongoing basis, and all names that are clearly inactive—due to death, change in residence, personal request, or nonrenewal over a period of at least five years—should be removed.

## Telefundraising

The process of telefundraising or phone solicitation, to secure donations is similar to the direct-mail process but can be more personal and effective, though more expensive. Generally speaking, phone solicitation can cost 50 cents out of each dollar raised and even more on acquisition calls.

The concept of telefundraising goes beyond simply conducting an end of the year phonathon, where the institution's staff and volunteers call all donors who have not yet renewed. Sophisticated telefundraising as an integral part of the campaign often requires the help of a consultant, who will develop the phoning schedule and budgets, create the telephone script, hire and train the callers, and record and tabulate the results. Consultants with larger firms often map out a campaign with a client and then assign an on-site captain or staff manager to run the campaign on a day-to-day basis. If the campaign is large and continuous, it may be useful to hire one consultant for a full year to alternate between telefundraising and telemarketing (phoning for the purpose of selling subscriptions, for example), sharing expenses with the marketing department.

There are at least five types of calls made, including (1) the renewal call, to an existing donor who has been written to but who has not responded; (2) the participant call, to an individual who has made multiple purchases of the primary product or service of the organization, such as a subscription, but has not yet contributed; (3) the single purchaser call, to a person who has made one purchase, but who has not made a contribution; (4) the mailing list call, to someone who has signed up for the mailing list but has not participated in the institution as either a purchaser or a donor; and (5) the cold call to an individual whose name was acquired through other lists.

### Scheduling and Budgeting

Scheduling is a crucial part of the phone campaign. The telefundraising campaign schedule should be integrated into the overall development campaign and complement rather than compete with direct-mail efforts, galas, and subscription drives.

When scheduling calls to the various groups, it is important to "hit the hot lists first." In other words, call lapsed donors soon after their donations are due and call subscribers or single-ticket buyers soon after they have attended events. The longer the institution waits, the harder it will be to maintain a person's interest in the institution.

Budgeting is usually based on the consultant's fee, the staff manager or site captain's fee, and the number of callers needed (callers are usually paid by the hour). Sometimes there may be additional computer costs incurred in tabulating the results of large campaigns. It is also often wise to give callers an incentive by offering to increase their salaries based on their success rate.

### Hiring and Training Callers

The number of callers required will obviously be based on the number of calls that need to be made and the timetable planned for the campaign. Callers should be interviewed by the staff manager to assure that their phone personalities reflect the image that the institution wishes to project. The phone captain will run regular training sessions for new callers to familiarize them with the work of the institution and demonstrate how to be effective callers. The phone captain will monitor each caller's progress every night. The captain must have the ability to remove those callers who cannot maintain minimum quotas.

## Creating and Using the Phone Script

First and foremost, it is important that the caller be sincere, courteous, and enthusiastic about "selling" the institution. The phone script is prepared ahead of time, and the callers have an opportunity to familiarize themselves with the script during the training session. For renewals, the script is usually quite simple, since the donor is already knowledgeable about the organization. However, it is a good idea to find out the donor's response to the institution's recent programs and acquire current address information. Renewal calls serve primarily as a reminder to supporters that their contribution is due.

The acquisition script is more complex and requires the presentation of more information, while being general enough not to confuse the listener with a barrage of details. The script provides the essential facts about the institution: its mission, a summary of its most successful programs, important new developments, and why contributions are vital.

The script also provides the caller with answers for the most common questions and listener responses, as well as instructions on how to record credit card information and other important facts about the new donor (see Appendix I, "Telefundraising Renewal Script" and Telefundraising Acquisition Script," for examples).

Telefundraising staff should also be trained to deal with objections from those being solicited. Pre-determined responses to objections frequently raised can accompany the script (see Appendix I, "Telefundraising Objection Responses").

## Recording and Tabulating Results

Telefundraising results should be tabulated in the following ways:

- Weekly results
- Comparative weekly results—evaluate one week against others for the campaign
- Total results for the entire campaign

All of the reports should document the number of donations paid by credit card and those pledged to be paid by check. The revenues generated by the calls should be compared against expenses in order to reflect the cost per gift and overall net revenue of the campaign. The report should also compute the amount of the average gift, the number of staff hours used, the average dollar amount raised per hour, the number of positive and negative responses, and the percentage of positive responses in relation to the total number of calls. Responses are divided into acquisition and renewal calls in order to provide the clearest, most specific information about the success of the campaign (see Chart 6.3, the telefundraising results report).

## CHART 6.3  TELEFUNDRAISING RESULTS REPORT

|  | TOTAL | CAMPAIGN TOTAL | |
|---|---|---|---|
|  |  | ACQUISITION | RENEWAL |
| **REVENUE** | | | |
| Credit Card - Paid: | # | | |
|  | $ | | |
| Checks - Pledged: | # | | |
|  | $ | | |
| TOTAL: | # | | |
|  | $ | | |
| Average Gift | | | |
| Staff Hours | | | |
| Avg. $ per Hour | | | |
| Yes Response | | | |
| No Response | | | |
| % Yes Response | | | |
| **EXPENSE** | | | |
| Staff Managers | | | |
| Callers' Payroll | ____ | ____ | ____ |
| TOTAL | | | |
| Cost per Gift | | | |
| Exp/Rev (Cents on the $) | | | |
| Net Revenue (Pledged) | | | |
| Unpaid Pledges | | | |
| Net Revenue (Actual) | | | |
| Projected Net Revenue* | | | |

*Assumes 85% fulfillment on pledged contributions. This chart was developed by Phil Reynolds.

## EVALUATING THE SUCCESS OF THE CAMPAIGN

The direct-mail and telefundraising campaigns should be evaluated at the conclusion of the fiscal year in a final report that answers the following questions:

- How much money was raised?
- How much money was spent?
- What was the net financial gain or loss from the direct-mail and telefundraising efforts?
- How many donors renewed their gifts?

- How many donors increased their gifts?
- How much money was brought in by donor renewals?
- How many new donors were acquired?
- How much money did new gifts generate?
- Which lists produced the best results?

The report should conclude with a paragraph outlining the major strengths and weaknesses of the campaign and recommendations for the future.

# Chapter 7
# Government

Government support to arts and cultural organizations is available at the federal and state levels and in some cases through municipal governments and community agencies. An organization's ability to secure funds at each level depends to a large degree on the quality of its programs and the audience it reaches. As with corporate, foundation, and individual funding sources, an organization is most likely to receive support from those government sources closest to home—local and state agencies.

State arts and humanities agencies have become increasingly significant sources of government support for most cultural organizations in America. As a group, the state agencies provide support to many more organizations than the National Endowment for the Arts or the National Endowment for the Humanities, the primary source of arts and cultural funding at the federal level. For many organizations, the chance of receiving funds at the state level is far greater, and the average program grant awarded often larger, than at the federal level. For these two reasons alone, arts and cultural organizations should establish close ties with their state agencies early in their fundraising efforts.

Identifying and approaching support programs at the community level should also be one of the first steps in an organization's search for funding. Depending on the locality, community support programs can provide significant funds. The community support programs in Houston and in Dallas–Fort Worth, for example, are major sources of support for local arts and cultural organizations. Some local agencies, however, provide technical and management assistance but offer no funds.

This chapter will discuss the major funding agencies at the federal level and will offer a general discussion of state agencies and community support programs.

## FEDERAL GOVERNMENT SUPPORT

During the Depression of the 1930s, the Works Progress Administration (WPA) provided jobs for unemployed artists through several programs. The Federal Theater Project, for instance, employed over 10,000 artists and helped launch the careers of many important actors and playwrights. These programs, however, were primarily designed to cope with unemployment rather than to support the arts.

During the next three decades, several events took place that increased Americans' awareness of the arts: World War II, one result of which was to bring Americans closer to Europe and its artistic traditions; the advent of television, which brought art and entertainment directly into the home; and the development of national tours for performing companies and art exhibits, which brought artistic activities to communities throughout the United States. During the same period, many community-based arts organizations were established across the country.

The first commitment made by the U.S. government to support a cultural activity took place in 1947, when a skeptical and reluctant Congress joined with private citizens to form the Smithsonian Institution. Nonetheless, broad government support for artistic endeavors was still many years away.

The government's role in fostering the growth of the arts was not clearly defined until 1965, when the National Foundation on the Arts and Humanities Act was passed. This act established the Federal Council on the Arts and Humanities and its operating agencies, the National Endowment for the Arts and the National Endowment for the Humanities.

The events leading to the passage of the law dated to the early 1950s, when Senator Hubert Humphrey first called for federal support of the arts. President John Kennedy also advocated support for culture and the arts, but he did not live long enough to bring about a formal procedure for providing funds. It was not until President Lyndon Johnson's administration that a mechanism was set up to disburse funds to the arts and humanities. In fact, the federal arts and cultural policy was in keeping with Johnson's Great Society legislation, and he became the primary advocate of a national cultural policy.

### The National Endowment for the Arts

The National Endowment for the Arts (NEA) was established in 1965, under the leadership of Roger Stevens, with a modest appropriation of $3 million. Following the election of Richard Nixon as president in 1968, Nancy Hanks was appointed to succeed Stevens and oversee a budget of $8.2 million. By late 1977, when Livingston L. Biddle, Jr., became chairman, the budget had increased to $114.6

million. Francis Hodsoll, who became chairman in November 1981, managed total appropriations for 1982 of $143 million, down from $159 million in fiscal year 1981. This represented the first reduction in government support of the arts since the Endowment was established in 1965. By 1988, however, the appropriation was $167 million, representing the highest to date.

The NEA provides financial support in the form of grants to individual artists and to not-for-profit organizations. The NEA also conducts research, provides information on the arts, acts as an advocate for the arts in the private sector, and works as a partner with state and local arts agencies to increase awareness of the arts among the general public.

Because of the influence the NEA has in supporting and funding arts activities, it is important for fundraisers to understand:

- The purpose and goals of the NEA
- How the NEA operates
- The grant programs of the NEA
- What types of support are available
- How to approach the NEA for funds

## Purpose and Goals

The purpose of the National Endowment for the Arts, as stated in its statement of mission, dated November 1986, is as follows:

The mission of the National Endowment for the Arts is to foster the excellence, diversity, and vitality of the arts in the United States, and to help broaden the availability and appreciation of such excellence, diversity, and vitality.

In implementing its mission the Endowment must exercise care to preserve and improve the environment in which the arts have flourished. It must not, under any circumstances, impose a single aesthetic standard or attempt to direct artistic content.

## How the NEA Operates

The NEA's basic organizational structure consists of:

- The National Council on the Arts
- Office of the chairman
- Office of the deputy chairman for programs
- Office of the deputy chairman for management
- Office of the deputy chairman for public partnership
- Program offices
- Advisory panels
- Regional offices

The National Council on the Arts is composed of 26 individuals who are widely recognized for their knowledge of, expertise in, or profound interest in the arts, and who have established records of distinguished service, or achieved eminence, in the arts. Council members are appointed by the president of the United States and serve six-year terms. The terms are staggered so that approximately one-third of the members are replaced every two years. The Council advises the chairman on policy matters and on decisions regarding grants. The Council holds four three-day meetings annually to consider applications, review guidelines, discuss major developments affecting any or all of the disciplines, and debate policy and program matters.

The chairman, who is also appointed by the president, is the official head of the NEA and is responsible for running the agency and making final decisions on grants and policies. This individual is, by law, the chairman of the National Council on the Arts.

The deputy chairman for programs, under the supervision of the chairman, is responsible for the management of the NEA's arts programs. The deputy chairman serves as principal advisor to the chairman on program matters and participates in formulating major policies of the agency. The deputy chairman for management supervises administration. The deputy chairman for public partnership is in charge of activities that relate to all state and local arts agencies as well as the Arts in Education Program.

There is a program office with a program director representing each of the following areas: dance, design arts, expansion arts, folk arts, inter-arts, arts programs, literature, media arts, museums, music, theater, opera–musical theater, and visual arts. The program directors are the primary links between the NEA and arts organizations and artists. The program directors and their staffs help organizations understand and comply with the NEA's grant-making policies and application processes. They also provide advice, information, and assistance as needed.

Advisory panels, which vary in size depending on the needs in each field, are made up of individuals with knowledge and expertise in each program area. Collectively, these individuals have knowledge and expertise in many different areas of a particular discipline. The panelists are selected from all parts of the country to serve on two kinds of panels: policy or overview panels, which develop and review guidelines and consider future plans for the programs; and grant panels, which review grant applications and make funding recommendations and may also review policy and guidelines. The chairman and the deputy chairman for programs appoint members of the advisory panels, who generally serve for a minimum of one year and a maximum of three years. Panelists are not full-time employees of the agency, but serve as needed, attending meetings throughout the year.

Six regional representatives are employed by the NEA to act as liaisons between the agency and the artists and arts groups in each region. Regional representatives are responsible for communicating to their constituents the goals, policies, application procedures, and programs of the agency.

## The NEA Grant Programs

The NEA provides support to arts organizations and individual artists in various fields through 13 grant programs. The November 1987 *Guide to the National Endowment for the Arts* describes the grant programs as follows:

> *Dance:* The Dance Program provides support for professional choreographers, dance companies, and organizations that present and serve dance. The Program funds all forms of professional dance. The Program does not fund general operating support, construction or renovation of facilities, scholarships, the completion of academic degrees, recreational or non-professional dance activities, and awards and/or competitions leading to awards. Generally, the Program does not fund the creation of new organizations, purchase of permanent equipment (unless rental exceeds purchase cost), publications other than catalogues or newsletters, dance training, student performing groups, or foreign travel.

> *Design Arts:* The Design Arts Program promotes excellence in the fields of architecture, landscape architecture, urban design, historic preservation, urban planning, interior design, industrial design, graphic design, and fashion design. This is done through grants and leadership initiatives that have the potential for producing results of exceptional merit and national or regional significance. Grants are awarded to professional designers; other qualified individuals working on innovative design projects; non-profit, tax-exempt organizations, including community or neighborhood organizations; arts groups and institutions; and colleges and universities, as well as local and state governments or any branch of these governments.

> *Expansion Arts:* The Expansion Arts Program supports professionally directed arts organizations of high artistic quality that are deeply rooted in and reflective of the culture of a minority, inner-city, rural, or tribal community. Funds are available to help create, exhibit, or present work reflective artistically of the culture of a community, to provide a community with access to all types of quality art, and to help train talented persons aspiring to be professional artists. Support is also available for program management, promotion, and documentation.

> *Folk Arts:* The Folk Arts Program supports the traditional arts that have grown through time within the many groups that make up

our nation—groups that share the same ethnic heritage, language, occupation, religion, or geographic area. These folk arts include music, dance, poetry, tales, oratory, crafts, and various types of visual art forms. The Program's main objectives are to preserve and enhance this multi-cultural artistic heritage and to make it more available to a wider public.

*Inter-Arts:* The Inter-Arts Program supports projects and institutions that cross the lines of individual art disciplines. The Program funds presenting organizations, artists' colonies, and service organizations, as well as interdisciplinary projects involving original work by artists from a variety of disciplines.

*Literature:* The Literature Program assists individual creative writers and literary translators, encourages wider audiences for contemporary literature, and assists non-profit literary organizations. The Program does not fund commercial presses or magazines, student publications, organizational newsletters, scholarly writing, regular curricula of educational institutions, completion of college or graduate degrees, faculty salaries, journalism, vanity or self-publication.

*Media Arts:* The Media Arts: Film/Radio/Television Program provides support to individual artists working in these media and to non-profit organizations that help artists carry out their projects. The Program defines the media arts broadly to include documentary, experimental, and narrative works, as well as electronic image manipulation, animated film, and audio art. The Program also offers funding for a limited number of major public television and radio series that bring other art forms to a wide public.

*Museums:* The Museum Program funds projects of artistic significance in the museum field. All types of museums, as well as some other organizations and museum professionals, are eligible for grants. In general, an organization must have been in operation for at least two years before submitting an application. The Program does not fund new construction or major structural modification of buildings.

*Music:* The Music Program provides support for the creation and performance of music, with an emphasis on assisting the growth of American music and musicians. Through its various categories, the Program awards grants to individuals of exceptional talent and to a wide range of performing, presenting, career development, and service organizations of the highest artistic level and of national or regional importance. Specific program guidelines exist in booklet form.

*Opera–Musical Theater:* The Opera–Musical Theater Program assists all forms of music theater generally involving voice—from experimental musical theater to operetta, from ethnic musical theater to classic musical comedy, from grand opera to still-developing forms. Grants support professional opera and musical theater producing organizations; the creation, development, rehearsal and production of new American or seldom produced works; regional touring; special projects; national and regional service organizations; and projects by individual producers.

*Theater:* The Theater Program provides financial assistance for the creation and presentation of work by professional artists, primarily in companies; for the development of the most talented individual artists; for touring of theater; for professional training; and for other activities that improve the environment in which artistic excellence can occur.

*Visual Arts:* The Visual Arts Program awards fellowships to individuals of exceptional talent working in a wide range of styles and media. It also awards matching grants to organizations that assist visual artists and supports public art projects and other activities that encourage dialogue about contemporary art.

The NEA office for public partnership administers the following programs that provide support to various artists, arts organizations, and arts agencies:

*Arts in Education Program:* The Arts in Education Program is a partnership program that is planned, administered, and financed through cooperative efforts of the Arts Endowment, state arts and education agencies, local communities, and education, arts education, and cultural institutions and organizations. The program's overall goal is to advance the arts as part of basic education.

*State programs:* All 50 states and six U.S. special jurisdictions (such as Guam and the District of Columbia) have official state arts agencies. With the exception of the private Vermont Council on the Arts, all are agencies of state government. In addition, the states have formed seven regional groups to administer programs and services most efficiently carried out on a multi-state basis. Grants go to assist designated state agencies and regional groups in carrying out plans for support of the arts.

*Local programs:* Local programs provide assistance to local arts agencies, state arts agencies, service organizations, colleges, and universities for projects that encourage increased and sustained support for the arts by local government and that strengthen local arts agencies as mechanisms for arts planning, financial support, services, and development at the local level.

There two other offices at the NEA that offer services and/or funds to specific groups. The Office of Special Constituencies helps to make the arts more available and accessible to handicapped individuals, senior citizens, veterans, and those confined in prisons, hospitals, or psychiatric institutions. The Arts Administration Fellows Program offers 13-week residencies at the NEA to arts administrators.

**Types of Support Available**

The NEA makes most of its grants through the program offices. The grants offered are determined by each particular program office based on the needs of the artistic discipline and the particular grantee. The following types of support are available:

*Matching grants*: All grants awarded to arts organizations through the various arts programs are made on a matching basis. Matching funds are not required for grants made to individuals. Generally, the matching requirement means that the organization must raise at least 50 percent of the costs of a given project, equaling the amount of the NEA grant. For example, if a project costs $15,000, the organization must raise at least $7,500 from other sources; the organization can request no more than one-half, or $7,500 in this case, of the total project costs from the NEA. Permissible sources of matching income are grants from private sources, revenues from ticket sales or other income-producing activities, and the value of project-related in-kind services.

*Challenge grants*: For the past decade the Challenge Grant Program has provided opportunities for arts institutions to strengthen their long-range institutional capacity and stability. Programs include: (1) Challenge III, which supports new or substantially augmented projects that address one or more of the following objectives: artistry, access, and appreciation; (2) Challenge II, which provides an opportunity for arts institutions of the highest artistic level to launch major fundraising campaigns that strengthen long-term institutional capacity and enhance artistic quality; and (3) The Advancement Program, which is designed to help organizations of the highest artistic excellence develop specific strategies to eliminate deficiencies in organizational management practice and take carefully planned steps toward the achievement of long-range goals.

The NEA challenge grants require a three-to-one match with the exception of awards for capital projects, which require a four-to-one match. The amount of time the recipient organization has to raise the matching funds varies from one to four years. The NEA also stipulates that challenge grant matching funds raised by the organizations must come from new and increased monies. Because these grants are more complex, organizations are advised to consult the challenge grant guidelines closely.

*Fellowships*: These grants, usually available only to U.S. citizens and permanent residents, are awarded to individuals of exceptional artistic talent for the purpose of developing their work.

*Treasury Fund grants*: Treasury Fund grants, designed to help applicants increase or sustain nonfederal contributions, generally must be matched with at least three nonfederal dollars for each federal dollar. They are not available for projects or in amounts different from those specified in the regular guidelines. The process of applying for and receiving Treasury Fund grants is similar to that for Program Fund grants. The amount requested from the Endowment, however, may not exceed 25 percent of the total project cost. The release of federal funds is contingent upon the following: (1) an applicant's securing, and documenting for the Endowment, pledges and/or private donations at least equal to the amount of federal funds; and (2) the approval by the Endowment of this documentation. This is referred to as the first match. The remaining minimum project cost (at least double the federal monies) must be met with additional matching funds secured by the grantee organization. For example:

| | |
|---|---|
| Endowment grant | $20,000 |
| First match by applicant | $20,000 |
| Additional matching by applicant | $40,000 |
| Minimum project cost | $80,000 |

Organizations interested in applying for a Treasury Fund grant are urged to contact the program before applying.

## How to Approach the NEA for Funds

Very detailed funding guidelines for each NEA program are published annually. In these guidelines, prospective grantees can find information on the application process and deadlines, typical grant sizes, eligibility requirements, and the program areas for which funds are available. The first step in approaching the NEA for funds is to obtain a copy of the guidelines from the appropriate program office. It is very helpful to meet and establish a working relationship with the director and other staff members of the NEA program to which the organization will apply most often.

It is also a good idea to add the appropriate NEA program directors and staff to the organization's mailing list and to keep them well informed of activities throughout the season. After an organization has applied for an NEA grant, the key staff should bring the NEA directors and staff up-to-date through a personal visit. Grant recipients should make it a point to visit NEA staff annually.

The NEA has defined a number of overall eligibility requirements with which all organizations must comply in order to receive funds. It should be noted that each funding program may have additional funding requirements that prospective grantees must meet. The NEA requires that prospective grant recipients be:

- Tax-exempt; that no private stockholder or individual may benefit from the net earnings of the organization; and that charitable donations are allowable as decreed under section 170(c) of the IRS Code of 1954 as amended.
- In compliance with Title VI of the 1964 Civil Rights Act, Title IX of the Education Amendment of 1974, and Section 504 of the Rehabilitation Act of 1974. Generally speaking, these laws prohibit discrimination on the basis of sex, race, religion, personal handicap, or national origin.
- In compliance with parts 3, 5, and 50(s) of Title 29 of the Code of Federal Regulations requiring appropriate compensation for all professional personnel, laborers, and mechanics.

In most cases, the organization must also have some track record and a demonstrated ability to produce quality programs in order to receive NEA funds.

To apply for funds, the development director should complete an official NEA application form. This form must be submitted with the specified materials prior to the application deadline. The program guidelines provide step-by-step instructions for completing the form (refer to Chart 7.1). Once the application has been submitted, it passes through various channels before a decision is made. Chart 7.2 illustrates the route the application takes at the NEA. The application is reviewed in the following manner:

1. The NEA program office reviews each application to make sure it is complete and then sends it on to the advisory panel for recommendation.
2. The advisory panel reviews the application and decides either to reject it or to award funds of a specified amount. Panel recommendations are then presented to the chairman and National Council.
3. The National Council reviews the panel's decision and presents its recommendations to the chairman for approval.
4. The chairman reviews the National Council's remarks and makes final decisions. Notifications of awards are sent to the arts organization selected to receive grants.
5. The applicant signs and returns a copy of the award letter, indicating acceptance of the grant.
6. The applicant requests the funds from the grants office according to the conditions of the grant, i.e., cash advance or

# CHART 7.1  HOW TO FILL OUT AN NEA APPLICATION FORM

| Inter-Arts Program Fiscal Year 1988 | Organization Grant Application Form NEA-3 (Rev.) Submit the original and three copies of this form to: Information Management Division/INTARTS, 8th floor, National Endowment for the Arts, Nancy Hanks Center, 1100 Pennsylvania Avenue, N.W., Washington, D.C. 20506. |
|---|---|

| I. Applicant Organization (name, address, zip) [The name by which you have received your tax exempt status under the IRS code section 501(c)(3). Project Director: Telephone: | II. Category under which support is requested: ☐ Presenting Organizations   ☐ Grants to Presenting Organizations   ☐ Services to Presenting Organizations ☐ Interdisciplinary Arts Projects ☐ Artists' Colonies ☐ Services to the Arts ☐ Arts Management Initiative | III. Period of support requested: Starting   [First Expense]       month   day   year Ending   [Final Expense]       month   day   year |
|---|---|---|

**IV. Summary of project description (Complete in space provided. Please DO NOT use photoreduction to fit more words into this space.)**

[This summary should be a clear, concise description of the project for which you are requesting support.

The first sentence should explicitly state the goals of the project. Subsequent sentences should outline objectives and results to be realized by the successful completion of the project. They should substantiate the need for the project, include the number of people to be served, and outline the method of evaluation.

It is vital that the project description be typed, and that it be neat, accurate, and complete. Remember that the description is often the most important element of the written application.

Do not continue this description on additional pages, unless the guidelines clearly direct you to do so.]

**V. Estimated number of persons expected to benefit from this project.** [Be sure to fill this in.]

**VI. Summary of estimated costs (recapitulation of budget items in Section IX)**

Total costs of project (rounded to nearest ten dollars)

[Total costs for this project only.]

A. Direct costs
  Salaries and wages      $ _____
  Fringe benefits
  Supplies and materials
  Travel
  Permanent equipment
  Fees and other
               Total costs   $ _____
B. Indirect costs  [Use only if you have a rate negotiated with a federal agency.]   $ _____
                   Total project costs   $ _____

**VII. Total amount requested from the National Endowment for the Arts** [No more than one-half of total project cost.]   $ _____
  NOTE: This amount (Amount requested):   $ _____
  PLUS Total contributions, grants, and revenues (X., page 3):   + _____
  MUST EQUAL Total project costs (VI. above):   = _____

**VIII. Organization total fiscal activity**      1986–87        1987–88 Est.
  A. Expenses    $ _____    $ _____
  B. Contributions, grants, and revenues    $ _____    $ _____

**Do not write in this space**

PYS: $

## CHART 7.1  HOW TO FILL OUT AN NEA APPLICATION FORM (continued)

IX. Budget breakdown of summary of estimated costs                                                                2

  A. Direct costs

    1. Salaries and wages

| Title and/or type of personnel | Number of personnel | Annual or average salary range | % of time devoted to this project | Amount $ |
|---|---|---|---|---|
| [Personnel for whom you withhold taxes; those paid on | | | | |
| an hourly or daily basis, such as consultants, should be | | | | |
| listed under "Other," Section IX, #5. | | | | |
| Annual salary x percentage of time = amount. | | | | |
| (Be careful if your project is for less than a year.)] | | | | |
| | | | | |
| | | | | |
| | | | | |

|  |  |
|---|---|
| Total salaries and wages | $ _____ |
| [usually 15%–20%] Add fringe benefits | $ _____ |
| Total salaries and wages including fringe benefits | $ _____ |

    2. Supplies and materials (list each major type separately)                                    Amount $

| | Amount $ |
|---|---|
| [Consumable supplies, such as paper, pens, etc; | |
| equipment costing less than $500 per unit.  Items | |
| costing more than $500 are entered under "Permanent Equipment," Section IX, #4.] | |
| Total supplies and materials | $ _____ |

    3. Travel

**Transportation of personnel**                                                                    Amount

| No. of travelers | from | to | $ |
|---|---|---|---|
| [This expense can be estimated according to the | | | |
| applicant's established travel practice, provided | | | |
| that the travel cost is reasonable.] | | | |
| | | | |
| Total transportation of personnel | | | $ _____ |

**Subsistence**

| No. of travelers | No. of days | Daily rate | $ |
|---|---|---|---|
| | | | |
| | | | |
| | | | |
| | | | |
| | | | |
| | | | |

|  |  |
|---|---|
| Total subsistence | $ _____ |
| Total travel | $ _____ |

# CHART 7.1  HOW TO FILL OUT AN NEA APPLICATION FORM (continued)

**3**

IX. Budget breakdown of summary of estimated costs (continued)

    4. Permanent equipment

| | Amount $ |
|---|---|
| [Each item costing $500 or more, with an estimated | |
| life of one year or more.] | |
| **Total permanent equipment** | $ |

    5. Fees for services and other expenses (list each item separately)

| | Amount $ |
|---|---|
| [Rent, utilities, telephone, rental of equipment, | |
| copying expense, and Other: consultants, hourly | |
| employees, printing, advertising, postage.  Anything | |
| else that is not in section I through IV.] | |
| | |
| | |
| **Total fees and other** | $ |

    B. Indirect costs   [If no rate has been established, itemize general administrative
        costs under sections I through III and leave this item   **Amount**
Rate established by attached rate negotiation agreement with
National Endowment for the Arts or another Federal agency   blank.]
Rate_____ %  Base $ _____

              $ _____

X. Contributions, grants and revenues (for this project)

    A. Contributions

        1. Cash

| | Amount $ |
|---|---|
| [Operating budget, indirect costs, salaried employees, | |
| donations, etc.] | |
| | |
| | |

        2. In-kind contributions (list each major item)

| | |
|---|---|
| [Donated time, space, supplies, etc.  These must be listed | |
| as expenses in the budget breakdown.] | |
| | |
| | |
| **Total contributions** | $ |

    B. Grants (do not list anticipated grant from the Arts Endowment)

| | |
|---|---|
| [Anticipated, not necessarily received.] | |
| | |
| | |
| **Total grants** | $ |

    C. Revenues

| | |
|---|---|
| [From this project only.] | |
| | |
| | |
| **Total revenues** | $ |
| **Total contributions, grants, and revenues for this project** | $ |

## CHART 7.1 HOW TO FILL OUT AN NEA APPLICATION FORM (continued)

---

XI. State Arts Agency notification       **4**

The National Endowment for the Arts urges you to inform your State Arts Agency of the fact that you are submitting this application.

Have you done so? \_\_\_\_\_ [XX] \_\_\_\_\_ yes _____ no

---

XII. Final Reports

Have you submitted required Final Report packages on all completed Inter-Arts Program grants since (and including) Fiscal Year 1984?

\_\_\_\_\_ Yes \_\_\_\_\_ No. If no, please mail immediately, under separate cover, to Grants Office/Final Reports Section to maintain eligibility. Do not include with your application package.

---

XIII. Certification

We certify that the information contained in this application, including all attachments and supporting materials, is true and correct to the best of our knowledge.

Authorizing official(s)    [Person with authority to legally bind the organization.]

Signature     X _____ Date signed _____
Name (print or type)
Title (print or type)     [President, Chair of the Board, or Executive Director]
Telephone (area code)

Signature     X _____ Date signed _____
Name (print or type)
Title (print or type)     [Treasurer or Comptroller]
Telephone (area code)

Project director

Signature     X _____ Date signed _____
Name (print or type)
Title (print or type)     [Executive Director or Director]
Telephone (area code)

*Payee (to whom grant payments will be sent if other than authorizing official)

Signature     X _____ Date signed _____
Name (print or type)
Title (print or type)
Telephone (area code)

*If payment is to be made to anyone other than the grantee, it is understood that the grantee is financially, administratively, and programmatically responsible for all aspects of the grant and that all reports must be submitted through the grantee.

---

BE SURE THAT YOUR APPLICATION PACKAGE INCLUDES ALL MATERIALS OUTLINED IN THE "HOW TO APPLY" SECTION FOR YOUR CATEGORY. LATE APPLICATIONS WILL BE REJECTED.

INCOMPLETE APPLICATIONS ARE UNLIKELY TO BE FUNDED.

---

Privacy Act
The Privacy Act of 1974 requires us to furnish you with the following information:
The Endowment is authorized to solicit the requested information by Section 5 of the National Foundation on the Arts and the Humanities Act of 1965, as amended. The information is used for grant processing, statistical research, analysis of trends, and for congressional oversight hearings. Failure to provide the requested information could result in rejection of your application.

---

Explanatory text developed by Timothy McClimon.

## CHART 7.2 NEA APPLICATION GRANT PROCESS

# NATIONAL ENDOWMENT FOR THE ARTS    WASHINGTON D.C. 20506

### APPLICATION/GRANT PROCESS

| APPLICANT/ GRANTS | ENDOWMENT OFFICES | ADVISORY PANELS | NATIONAL COUNCIL ON THE ARTS | PROCEDURE |
|---|---|---|---|---|
| | ● | | | Program Director, in consultation with advisory panel members/experts in the field, National Council on the Arts, and the Chairman of the National Endowment for the Arts, prepares Guidelines announcing grant programs, eligibility for application, application deadlines. |
| ● | | | | Grant program announcements and Guidelines are published, provided to all organizations of known capability, and distributed to a wide mailing list, which includes libraries and press outlets. The Arts Endowment also publishes and distributes the Guide to the National Endowment for the Arts. Brief descriptions of all Programs are published in the annual Catalog of Federal Domestic Assistance sold by the Government Printing Office. |
| | ● | | | Potential applicants respond to program announcements and request Guidelines with application forms if they do not already have them. |
| ● | | | | Program Offices or Public Information Office responds to requests and provides Application Guidelines to potential applicants. Applicants review Guidelines and prepare the formal applications. |
| | ● | | | Applicants submit formal applications. Copy of IRS letter, attesting to an organization's tax–exempt status, must accompany application. |
| | ◉ | | | Applications are reviewed by Program Offices to make sure materials are complete. Reviewed applications are presented to advisory panels for review and recommendation. |
| | | ◉ | | Advisory panels, whose members are professionals from the field, review all applications that fall within the Program Guidelines and comply with the required eligibility and IRS status. Panels recommend those applications to be funded and those to be rejected. |
| | ● | | | Panel suggestions can be incorporated into the proposed grant. Sometimes, for example, an applicant's budget must be revised; and in these cases, the panel comments are reviewed with the applicant by the Program staff. |
| | | | ◉ | Applications, with all panel recommendations for funding and rejection, are presented to the 26 member National Council on the Arts, which reviews the applications again and makes further recommendations. |

## CHART 7.2 NEA APPLICATION GRANT PROCESS (continued)

| APPLICANT/ GRANTS | ENDOWMENT OFFICES | ADVISORY PANELS | NATIONAL COUNCIL ON THE ARTS | PROCEDURE |
|---|---|---|---|---|
| | ● | | | The Chairman, on the basis of recommendations from the National Council on the Arts, approves the applications for assistance. Program Offices, in consultation with the Grants Office, prepare grant letters for the Chairman's signature. The Chairman, or his designate signs grant award letters signifying approval of the grants. (Program Directors send letters to rejected applicants.) |
| ● | | | | A signed grant letter is forwarded to potential grantee. |
| ● | | | | Grantee submits initial request to Grants Office for cash payment and by signing signifies acceptance of the grant and its conditions. Subsequent payments are submitted in accordance with terms of the grant. |
| | ● | | | Grants Office staff reviews request for each cash payment. |
| ● | | | | Cash payments are authorized and forwarded to grantee. |
| ● | | | | Grantee completes project and submits Final Descriptive and Expenditure Reports to the Grants Office. |
| | ● | | | Staff reviews and approves final reports and closes out grant. |
| ● | | | | Audit of grantee is conducted, if appropriate. |

● = Operation: To prepare or refer to document. To complete an application for example.

◉ = Review: To check an application or report for quality, accuracy and compliance.

reimbursement. The appropriate form is completed and mailed to the NEA.

7. Payments are authorized by the NEA and mailed to the grantee.
8. A final report describing in narrative form the outcome of the project and accompanying fiscal documentation is sent to the grants office by the organization at the completion of the funding year.
9. The final report is approved by the NEA staff and the grant is concluded.

Following is a discussion of other federal agencies that have provided funds to arts organizations for specific projects. Organizations interested in obtaining funds from these agencies should thoroughly investigate them before applying.

## The National Endowment for the Humanities

The National Endowment for the Humanities (NEH) was established in 1965 along with the NEA to support research, education, and public programs in the humanities, fields such as history, philosophy, linguistics, languages, literature, archaeology, jurisprudence, ethics, education, comparative religion, and the history and criticism of the arts.

The NEH, which in 1989 has an appropriation of $140.4 million, funds both not-for-profit institutions and individuals and expects its support to leverage other nonfederal dollars and to complement existing or planned private and local initiatives. The NEH generally supports scholarship and research in the humanities, the improvement of humanities education, and projects that foster in the American people a greater curiosity about and understanding of the humanities.

In order to provide a useful overview of the NEH, the following topics will be covered:

- How the NEH operates
- The grant programs of the NEH
- How to approach NEH for funds

### How the NEH Operates

The NEH's basic organizational structure consists of:

- The National Council on the Humanities
- The Office of the chairman
- The Office of the deputy chairman
- The Office of the assistant chairman for programs
- The Office of the assistant chairman for administration
- Offices for each humanities division
- Peer-review panels

This structure echos closely the structure of the NEA.

The actual awarding of grants occurs through the major program divisions, the staff of these divisions are the primary links to humanities organizations. The division staff recommends projects for funding after guiding applications through a peer review process. The final responsibility for awards rests with the chairman of the Endowment. The chairman is advised by a board of 24 private citizens who make up the National Council on the Humanities. These individuals serve six-year terms; the chairman, who is appointed by the president of the United States, serves for four years.

The peer-review process is provided by nearly 1,000 private scholars and professionals in the humanities, who serve on 150 panels annually. These individuals make judgments on each application, and these reviews are assembled by the NEH staff and then presented to the National Council. The Council meets four times a year to advise the chairman on the funding of applications. It is the chairman who makes the final decisions.

## The NEH Grant Programs

The NEH awards grants in the humanities through five program divisions and two program offices. Much of the following discussion on the NEH programs is based on "Overview of Endowment Programs," a very helpful document that can be obtained by calling the NEH directly.

*Division of Education Programs:* This division makes grants to organizations under two broad categories: (1) higher education and (2) elementary and secondary education. Activities supported include institutes, workshops, conferences, and curriculum development. Most successful projects are cooperative efforts among institutions.

*Division of Fellowships and Seminars:* It is from this division that individual teachers and scholars, as opposed to institutions, can obtain funds to conduct studies or other research and independent projects. Included are fellowships for university faculty, independent scholars, faculty members of historically black colleges or universities, and high school and college students. Travel grants and various stipends are also available.

*Division of General Programs:* The focus of grant making in this category is on increasing public understanding and appreciation of the humanities. Grants are generally made for exhibitions, radio and television programs, lectures, symposia, printed materials, and reading and discussion groups at libraries.

*Division of Research Programs:* Grants in this division support the preparation of important humanities works, collections, reference materials, research projects, and institutions that foster humanities research.

*Division of State Programs:* In a similar way to the NEA, this division provides support to state humanities councils in all 50 states, the District of Columbia, Puerto Rico, and the U.S. Virgin Islands.

*Office of Challenge Grants:* Humanities institutions engaged in seeking new sources of long-term support may apply for a challenge grant. Funds received, which must be matched on at least a three-to-one basis, must be used to establish or increase institutional endowments, to purchase capital equipment, or retire debt.

*Office of Preservation:* Grants from this office of NEH support efforts to preserve significant resources for the humanities, such as books, manuscripts, documents, newspapers, maps, photographs, film, sound recordings, and tape.

### How to Approach the NEH for Funds

As with the NEA, the first step in approaching the NEH for funds is to obtain the guidelines and application forms for the program area most suitable. The guidelines are fairly detailed, providing deadline dates, eligibility requirements, examples of successful grants, and instructions on how to apply. It is strongly recommended that a working relationship with an appropriate NEH staff member be established.

## The United States Information Agency

The United States Information Agency (USIA) sponsors international cultural exchange programs with foreign countries to promote greater understanding between U.S. citizens and other peoples of the world. For example, the USIA may help finance tours to the Soviet Union and the Far East or provide assistance to organizations arranging private tours abroad. The USIA administers the Fulbright Scholarships for student and teacher exchanges, and the Grant-in-Aid Program, which offers financial grants to the international programs of private organizations. Through the United States Information Service, the USIA also maintains cultural centers with extensive libraries in more than 95 countries to help foreign citizens learn more about the United States.

## The Institute of Museum Services

The Institute of Museum Services provides support to a broad range of museums, including botanical gardens, aquariums, planetariums, zoos, and arboretums, as well as for art, natural history, and science museums, among others. Grants are awarded to such organizations for operating expenses, conservation, the professional assessment of programs, facilities, and education programs. In fiscal year 1988, the Institute received appropriations totaling $21,944,000.

## Other Federal Agencies

There are a number of other government agencies that have in the past supported programs or projects in the arts. Among the agencies that have provided grants to arts organizations are the departments of Health, Education, and Welfare; Commerce; Housing and Urban Development; Defense; Interior; Labor; and Agriculture. Grants have also been given by the General Services Administration, the Corporation for Public Broadcasting, the Community Services Administration, and the National Trust for Historic Preservation.

The availability of funds from these agencies is largely dependent upon decisions made by the presidential administration currently in office. Interested development directors should determine the existence of grant programs in these agencies and investigate the application requirements and regulations before entering into a formal application procedure. Officials in congressional offices can be helpful in this process.

## STATE SUPPORT PROGRAMS

Support to the arts and humanities at the state level existed long before the federal government began to provide funding through the NEA and NEH. The federal agencies, however, were a major catalyst in the creation of official arts and culture funding agencies in almost every state.

### State Arts Councils

According to the NEA guidelines for state programs, "By law no less than 20 percent of the Endowment's program funds must be made available for grants to designated state arts agencies and regional groups of state arts agencies." These funds are awarded to state arts agencies and regional groups in the form of basic state grants and regional arts programming grants.

These block grants have provided a powerful incentive for local support and have inspired state legislatures to appropriate amounts that at least match the NEA allocation. The New York State Council on the Arts operated with state appropriations of $54 million in fiscal year 1988, making it the largest state arts agency in terms of total dollars awarded in grants. Massachusetts is second, with total appropriations of $21.7 million, and New Jersey third, with $19.9 million.

The overriding purpose of most state agencies is the development and support of artists, community arts activities, and arts organizations statewide. There are many similarities in the grant-making procedures of state agencies. For example, most state agencies have some kind of matching fund requirement. However, each state agency develops its own grant-making policies, programs, and application guidelines.

Most state agencies act as information resources for arts organizations and artists in the state. These agencies provide information on arts activities, publish annual lists of art fairs and festivals, and disseminate information relating to various kinds of technical and management assistance available.

Development personnel and other top management in arts organizations should develop a comfortable working relationship with the grants officer of the state arts agency. As does the NEA, most state agencies have clearly defined application forms, deadlines, and eligibility requirements for prospective grantees. An arts organization that serves a local community has a much stronger case for support at the state level than at the federal level because the state agency has tailored its programs to the unique cultural makeup of the state. The state agency also has a more intimate understanding of those organizations located within its boundaries. A local arts group appealing directly to the NEA, for instance, may have a difficult time justifying the need for federal funds, because federal funding programs are developed to meet nationwide priorities.

## State Humanities Councils

The founding legislation of the National Endowment for the Humanities provided for the distribution of a portion of its funds through state humanities councils. There are humanities councils in all 50 states, the District of Columbia, Puerto Rico, and the U.S. Virgin Islands. These councils differ from their counterpart state arts councils in that in many cases they are not agencies of state governments but rather committees of private citizens. Each state humanities council establishes its own grant guidelines and application deadlines. A wide variety of humanities projects are funded through state councils, including conferences, lectures, workshops, exhibits, media presentations, and scholars-in-residence programs.

## COMMUNITY SUPPORT PROGRAMS

There are approximately 2,000 community arts and culture agencies in the United States. The idea of establishing local councils for arts and culture first emerged in the 1950s. It is generally believed that the first community arts group in the United States was in Winston-Salem, North Carolina. Many of the community agencies are private, not-for-profit organizations, not branches of city or county governments.

The goals and programs of community groups and the ways in which they are organized reflect the unique makeup of their particular localities. The primary functions of most agencies include providing a local clearinghouse for cultural information, acting as cultural advocates in their home communities, and offering administrative and technical services in such areas as bookkeeping, fundraising, and publicity. In some cases, most typically in small towns, the local arts and cultural agency will produce or present all cultural activities in the community by sponsoring performing arts series, art exhibits, and film series and by organizing festivals and competitions.

Some community arts and cultural agencies actually make grants to local organizations and artists/scholars. Others conduct annual united fund drives among community businesses on behalf of local cultural organizations. Because they represent the larger interests of the community and tend to be more financially stable, community cultural agencies are often more effective than an individual organization in securing state and federal support.

Since community cultural agencies are in business to provide services to the cultural organizations in their localities, leaders of a cultural organization should develop a personal relationship with the management of the local agency.

# Chapter 8
# Special Events

Special events are activities other than the organization's usual fundraising programs that are undertaken for the purpose of raising money and generating public awareness of the organization. The types and number of special events should serve to enhance the overall fundraising campaign rather than compete with it. Special events have the potential, if undertaken properly, to generate substantial funds and cultivate prospects. The visibility associated with special events can also produce greater public awareness of the organization and its programs. Special events can often attract new board members and individual donors as well as serve to thank those who have already given.

Special events include business or community awards dinners, luncheons, celebrity benefit performances, marathons, auctions, and even bake sales. Events for cultivation may include inviting members of the state legislature and city council and their families to a private showing of an exhibition and cocktail party. Special events might also be tailored to attract new prospects within certain business sectors and industries, such as real estate, banking, or fashion.

An organization may choose to have several different kinds of special events throughout the year or one major annual function.

More than any other type of fundraising, special events require the participation of the organization's entire staff as well as many volunteers. In most cases, undertaking a special event also means planning a press and advertising campaign to generate visibility for the organization and publicity for the event itself. In addition, special events carry a great deal of risk because they may require a large outlay of money before the event occurs, with no guarantee of a return. Special events require the same dedication to planning and research, and the same commitment to participation by board members, as other types of fundraising carried out by the organization.

Organizations of any size can undertake a special event. Newly formed organizations will find special events a particularly helpful way to raise funds until an overall annual campaign has been established. The organization should resist the temptation to overspend; always remember that the event exists for the purpose of raising money. A detailed budget that has been carefully thought out and closely monitored by the development director will help keep expenses at a reasonable level.

Undertaking a special event entails:

- Choosing the special event
- Developing a leadership base
- Compiling the invitation list
- Designing the invitation package
- Making the sale
- Implementing the press campaign
- Working with caterers, designers, florists, and photographers
- Using consultants and volunteers
- Following up

## CHOOSING THE SPECIAL EVENT

Special events should reflect and enhance the image of the organization and should be appropriate to the community. For example, a small avant-garde music group will most likely produce a special event very different from one undertaken by a large opera company.

The nature of the community must also be considered when deciding upon the kind of event the organization will produce. Talent shows starring political personalities are popular in Washington, D.C., where politics plays a major role in daily life. Auctions can be successful in areas where local businesses and celebrities are willing to donate goods and services and where attendees are willing to spend money spontaneously. A rummage sale near Halloween that features bargains on a theater company's old costumes can be very effective, particularly in a community where there are limited commercial costume outlets. Large media events, such as television auctions, marathons, and award dinners featuring celebrities and business leaders, can generate a great deal of money but require months of planning, a substantial amount of staff time, and a broad leadership base.

Fundraising events, however, do not have to be complicated. Bake sales, family picnics, and parties in the homes of supporters are examples of simple but effective kinds of special events. In selecting an appropriate special event the organization must realistically assess the amount of money and staff time it is able to commit to the event.

Once the event has been selected, the organization must choose a date. The date should be determined well in advance and not conflict with other events in the community scheduled for the same day. The decision to hold an event on a weekend or a weekday evening will depend on the nature of the community and the type of event chosen.

Also, if a celebrity or community leader is to be honored, make certain that the person is available and will accept the award in person.

## THE LEADERSHIP BASE

Developing the leadership base is the most important step in producing a successful event. The leadership structure for a special event is a pyramid of prominent individuals with wide influence who will help generate funds through their prestige and glamour and through their encouragement of friends and colleagues to participate in the event. The selection of a chair of the special event is essential—the position requires an individual who has the clout to sell large numbers of tickets and who is willing to enlist colleagues to serve as vice-chairs.

Business executives and socially prominent individuals usually make ideal chairs. Since most businesses and corporations have public-relations budgets with funds allocated for community fundraising events, it is important to have a chair with prestige in the corporate sector. However, make sure that a potential chair has not worked on behalf of too many other organizations, in the process using up all existing "favors" from colleagues. Sometimes it is appropriate to have a corporate chair who will generate sales from the corporate world and a gala chair who generates support from social contacts.

A committee of vice-chairs is often named to expand the leadership base. Sometimes a chair will have a list of contacts so large and prestigious that only that person is needed to serve in a leadership capacity. In many cases, however, vice-chairs are needed to expand the base of support. To enlist vice-chairs for a special event, the organization asks board members, friends of the organization, or other prominent individuals in the community to serve. In addition, the chair of the event, writing on personal stationery, invites as many business and civic colleagues as possible to participate. Celebrities and political leaders should be asked to serve as either honorary chairs or as members of a special event committee. These individuals add prestige to the event.

## THE INVITATION LIST

Once the leadership base for the event has been recruited, invitation lists should be compiled consisting of the names of the persons that the chair of the event and the committee of vice-chairs would most likely know. For example, a vice-chair who is in the real estate business should be asked to provide a personal list as well as review a list of individuals in the realty community and related industries, such as construction.

Lists can be compiled by researching the membership rolls of the local chamber of commerce and business trade associations. The organization's donors, selected subscribers, friends of board members, and board members of other arts and humanities organizations should be considered as potential invitees. This process can be bypassed by hiring a consultant who already has accurate and up-to-date lists prepared. This service may be costly, but the quality of a consultant's lists may prove to be worth the expense.

Once the lists have been compiled, the chair and vice-chairs are asked to peruse the lists, deleting inappropriate names and adding others to whom invitations should be sent. The chair and vice-chairs must also identify individuals on the list whom they know on a first-name basis and suggest an appropriate salutation. The more personal the contact, the greater the possibility of an affirmative response. A business is most likely to purchase tickets when its top executive is asked to return a favor by a top executive at another business. Sometimes, however, a business will purchase tickets because of keen interest in the event itself, out of civic responsibility, or because the cultural organization is known by its key executives. After the lists have been reviewed, any names left unmarked for personal solicitation should be added to the chair's list and given a formal salutation.

It must be kept in mind that the members of the leadership committee are extremely busy individuals who have graciously accepted the responsibility of fundraising for the organization. Use their time efficiently and wisely. It is essential that the organization provide its chair and vice-chairs with accurate and well-researched lists that are easy to read. A poorly prepared list will not be read.

The lists should then be scrupulously checked to avoid duplication in mailing. An easy way to avoid this problem is to prepare a file card or computer record with the name, address, and place of business of each person invited. Note on the bottom of the card the initials of the member of the leadership committee who is sending the invitation. File the cards alphabetically by business affiliation, or by name when appropriate. This system also helps avoid inviting several officials in the same business. Since many corporations purchase blocks of tickets, it can be confusing for a company to receive more than one invitation. The invitation should be sent to the chair of the company or to the leadership committee member's primary contact. In some cases, it may be appropriate to invite more than one individual affiliated with a particular business, but it is necessary to let each invitee know of others being invited from the company and also who is doing the inviting.

## THE INVITATION PACKAGE

The invitation package should be mailed no less than seven or eight weeks before the event occurs. The package should include a carrier envelope, the invitation, a reply card and reply envelope, and a letter addressed either formally or informally. See Appendix I, "Special Event Invitation Package," for an example.

The chair and vice-chairs should send letters with invitations on their own stationery to individuals whom they know personally; special stationery designed for the event is often used to invite those individuals who are not personally known. The content of the invitation letter must be approved by the chair and vice-chairs before it is printed on their stationery. The letter should mention the writer's role as chair or vice-chair of the event and should include a description of the event, reasons why the event and organization should be supported, and general instructions on how to pledge support. The letter should close with a paragraph stating the writer's hope that the recipient will join him or her on the night of the event. The letter should be a concise but stirring appeal, making the reader feel it is his or her responsibility to accept. See Appendix I, "Special Event Invitation Package," for an example of such a letter.

The invitation must be simple and easy to comprehend. The date, time, place, and theme of the event should be featured on the cover. The invitation should list the names of the chair, honorary chair, vice-chairs, and celebrity committee members; it should also highlight the name of the honoree, if appropriate, and outline the order of events for the evening. In addition, it should describe how the proceeds will be used to help the organization and, if there is an honoree, indicate why that individual has been selected for an award.

The reply card, which can resemble the format of the invitation on a smaller scale, restates the theme, time, and place of the event. It should list the ticket prices and what the invitee is getting in return for purchasing a ticket or block of tickets at a particular price. For example, a business that buys a block of 10 tickets for $1,000 may be called a "patron," with each ticket holder entitled to cocktails, prime seating for the event, and dinner following the performance. A "sponsor" may be an organization purchasing 10 tickets for $500, entitling ticket holders to cocktails and preferred seating. Prices for individual tickets at each level should also be listed.

The reply form should include space for the purchaser to fill in name, address, place of business, and the number and price of tickets purchased. The percentage of the ticket that is tax deductible, as determined by law, should also be indicated, as well as instructions for making out the check. An additional line requesting a contribution—"I am unable to attend but enclose a contribution of $ _____ "—should also be placed on the reply form.

The names of the individuals who will actually be attending the event should also be requested in the reply card. This is done because blocks of tickets are often purchased by businesses or individuals, and it may be important for seating protocol to know the names of the guests. It can be embarrassing if empty seats are left at dinner tables or in the theater. Any unused tickets can be given to friends of the organization to fill the house.

Once the invitation package has been designed, it must be printed. Carrier envelopes should be printed first so that they can be addressed while the other parts of the invitation package are being printed. The body of the invitation letter can be printed in quantity on the appropriate stationery. The headings and salutations will have to be typed individually. However, the typeface must match that used in the body of the letter. This kind of individualized invitation is expensive, but it is more personal and therefore more effective than a "dear friend" letter.

Attention should be paid to the weight of the papers used so that the package conforms to first-class mailing regulations and does not add unnecessarily to the cost of the invitation package. First-class postage is recommended for special event invitations, as are hand-addressed or typed envelopes. Avoid using labels or window envelopes.

## MAKING THE SALE

Two or three weeks after the invitations have been mailed, staff members must telephone invitees who have not responded. When making these calls, the staff or volunteers should identify themselves as the representative of the chair or vice-chair who sent the invitation, thereby reinforcing the personal nature of the solicitation. Phone "pulls," as they are called, are time consuming and tedious, but they net positive results. Keep calling, being sure to wait a reasonable period of time between calls, until a definite yes or no is given unless you have been specifically asked not to.

## THE PRESS CAMPAIGN

The press campaign for a special event is crucial to its success. The campaign must be well planned and designed to reach potential ticket buyers; attention must be paid to the demographic profile of the audience a particular medium can reach. Promotion costs, however, should be kept to a minimum.

The organization should carefully weigh the pros and cons of buying newspaper, radio, or television advertising and producing posters and flyers to be circulated in the community. This type of promotion should be carefully targeted to reach the audience that can afford a special event ticket and is interested enough to purchase one. On the other hand, "free" press, including radio or television interviews and feature stories in arts or society newspaper columns, can be very helpful and should be taken advantage of by the organization.

## CATERERS, DESIGNERS, FLORISTS, AND PHOTOGRAPHERS

Special events often involve providing food for guests and creating a special atmosphere. Organizing the catering and decorations for an event can be a creative and enjoyable experience. It tends to be costly, however, so careful planning and budgeting is important. The development director would be wise to encourage the participation of the gala chair or representatives of this chair in this aspect of the event, as they will most likely be very knowledgeable about party planning.

Caterers should be asked to submit sample menus that are within the organization's budget and hold a tasting for the principal staff and leadership. It is common for caterers to submit a written proposal outlining their complete menu and bar set-up; a floorplan describing how the room will be laid out to ensure efficient service; the number of waiters and other service people required; a list of rental items that the organization may need; and, lastly, the terms for payment. Itemized prices for each component—food, service, rental items—should be included in the proposal.

If a florist and/or designer is to be hired, the organization should ask them for written plans or drawings if necessary. Once the caterer's and florist's proposals have been accepted, they should be rewritten in the form of a contract and signed by both parties. Musicians should also submit a contract indicating when and how long they are scheduled to play, the number of musicians and their instruments, and the costs of their services. It is also a good idea to hire a photographer. A photographic record of the evening may be useful in promoting the organization at a later time, particularly if celebrities and corporate, social, civic, and political leaders are present.

Before hiring anyone—florist, caterer, photographer, or designer— the organization should know all of the details regarding the vendors' plans for the event and should not be inhibited from requesting them. The individuals hired form the "production team" for the special event and must work well together to make the event a success. It is important that the development director supervise these individuals and provide them with realistic budget figures and adequate time for setting up, as well as an understanding of the facility and a thorough orientation to the organization and the purpose and nature of the event.

Guests at special events are usually paying a significant amount of money to attend and deserve to be treated well. If the evening is a success, it will be easier for the organization to sell tickets to future events.

## CONSULTANTS AND VOLUNTEERS

If volunteers are used, they must have a staff liaison working with them to ensure adequate communication between the development department and the volunteers. Volunteers should have specific assignments and deadlines for completing them. Responsibilities range from making telephone calls and greeting guests to actually planning and carrying out the entire event. Special events can be very rewarding for volunteers, but they must not be taken advantage of by the organization. The development director must be careful to give the volunteer a variety of tasks, depending on his or her interests.

Hiring special event consultants can be expensive but, under the right circumstances, extremely cost effective. Consultants from reputable firms will have excellent invitation lists and their own printer, lettershop, and phone-solicitation staff; they will also be able to produce and mail the invitations and make the follow-up telephone calls efficiently and easily. Consultants can also help to conceptualize the event, develop the budget, and assist in retaining a caterer, florist, and designer. They will keep the records of ticket purchases, meet with the leadership committee as needed, and help with seating arrangements if required. It is a good idea to check a consultant's references as well as attend one of the events the consultant has undertaken. In making the decision about whether to use a consultant, the organization's development director must first decide whether the staff and volunteers have the time and expertise to do the work a consultant can.

## THE FOLLOW-UP

After the event is over and thank you letters have been sent, do not forget to add the names of those who attended to the organization's mailing lists. Research the attendees for potential new board members or donors. Keep good records of the entire event so that the knowledge gained from this experience can be helpful in the future.

# Conclusion

As two working development directors, we are aware of the intense competition for contributed dollars and the financial struggle in which organizations must engage to create artistic work and cultural programming. We can only suggest, first and foremost, not to take rejection from funders personally. Try to maintain a sense of humor and calm amidst the frequent disappointments. Good fundraisers do not always succeed with every grant request but have the determination to continue. Endurance and a strong sense of self-worth are necessary qualities.

Because the fundraising profession is a stressful one, learning to cope with uncertainties is essential. Networking with other fundraisers can be very helpful as well as entertaining, especially when sharing "war stories."

Try very hard to negotiate attainable fundraising goals. Unrealistic projections are demoralizing and give the institution a false sense of security.

Some donors and prospects can be intimidating, and it is always helpful to remember that funders are people too. The real joy in doing this kind of work is the relationships and friendships formed that can enrich your life. Getting a grant is a personal and institutional success that can help create something of lasting value for society. We have found that the best fundraisers believe deeply in the institutions and causes for which they seek funds.

Good luck.

# Appendix A
# Basic Fundraising Books

*American Philanthropy*, Robert Bremner. Chicago: University of Chicago Press, 1960. Available from University of Chicago Press,
5801 South Ellis Avenue, Chicago, IL 60637.
An historical overview of the development of philanthropy from colonial
times to the present.

*America's Voluntary Spirit*, Brian O'Connell. New York: The Founda-
tion Center. Available from The Foundation Center, 79 Fifth
Avenue, New York, NY 10003.
A series of articles on the philosophy and impact of philanthropy in the
United States.

*Arts Money, Raising It, Saving It, and Earning It*, Joan Jeffries. New
York: Neal Schuman Publishers Inc., 1983. Available from Neal
Schuman Publishers Inc., 23 Corneraliu Street, New York, NY
10014.
A guide to fundraising techniques and strategies for arts organizations.

*CASE Matching Gift Details*. Washington, DC: Council for the Advancement and Support of Education. Available from CASE, Suite
400, 11 Dupont Circle, Washington, DC 20036.
Detailed descriptions of corporate matching grant programs including lists
of eligible organizations.

*Corporate Social Programs: Nontraditional Assistance*, Anne Klepper.
New York: The Conference Board, 1983. Available from The
Conference Board, 845 Third Avenue, New York, NY 10022.
A report on corporate non-cash giving programs compiled from a Con-
ference Board survey.

*The Direct Mail Lists Rates and Data Directory*. Wilmette, IL: Standard Rate and Data Service, biannual. Available from Standard
Rate and Data Service, 3004 Glenview Road, Wilmette, IL 60091.
A catalogue of mailing lists available for rent through list brokers, managers, or owners.

*Effective Corporate Fundraising*, W. Grant Brownrigg. New York:
American Council for the Arts, 1982. Available from American
Council for the Arts, 570 Seventh Avenue, New York, NY 10018.
Outlines an entire strategy for a nonprofit organization to approach cor-

porate funding prospects, including examples of letters, budgets, and a campaign calendar.

*Effective Leadership in Voluntary Organizations*, Brian O'Connell. New York: Walker and Co., 1981. Available from Walker and Co., 750 Fifth Avenue, New York, NY 10019.
A guide to nonprofit management, planning, and fundraising.

*Foundation Fundamentals*, edited by Patricia E. Read. Third Edition, New York: The Foundation Center, 1986. Available from The Foundation Center, 79 Fifth Avenue, New York, NY 10003.
A guide to foundation regulations and activities that includes a description of resources available to help grantseekers learn about foundations.

*Fund Raising for Museums: The Essential Book for Staff and Trustees.* Bellevue, WA: The Hartman Planning and Development Group, 1985. Available from The Hartman Planning and Development Group, P.O. Box 818, Redmond, WA 98073.
Basic instructions for museum fundraisers, including a directory of foundations, corporations, and government agencies that have funded museums.

*Fund Raising Letter Collection.* Plymouth Meeting, PA: The Fundraising Institute. Available from The Fundraising Institute, Box 365, Ambler, PA 19002.
A compilation of actual fundraising letters used by not-for-profit organizations in the United States.

*Giving USA. Annual Report.* New York: American Association of Fund Raising Counsel, Inc. Available from American Association of Fund Raising Counsel, Inc., 25 West 43rd Street, New York, NY 10036.
An annual statistical report and discussion of contributions made by corporations, foundations, and individuals to all types of U.S.-based not-for-profit organizations.

*The Golden Donors: A New Anatomy of the Great Foundations*, Waldemar A. Nielson. New York: E.P. Dutton, 1985. Available from E.P. Dutton, 2 Park Avenue, New York, NY 10016.
An analysis of the 36 largest private foundations in America, including founding donors, governance, and funding activities.

*Grants for the Arts*, Virginia P. White. New York: Plenum Publishing Corporation, 1980. Available from Plenum Publishing Corporation, 227 West 17th Street, New York, NY 10011.
A book designed to provide basic information on all aspects of seeking financial assistance for all the arts.

*The Grantsmanship Book.* Los Angeles: The Grantsmanship Center. Available from the Grantsmanship Center, 1015 West Olympic Boulevard, Los Angeles, CA 90015.
Compendium of articles providing practical advice on program planning, proposal writing, and funding strategies for nonprofit managers.

*The Grass Roots Fund Raising Book*, Joan Flanagan. Chicago: Contemporary Books, 1981. Available from National Office, The Youth Project, 1555 Connecticut Avenue, N.W., Washington, DC 20036.
Handbook providing practical advice on planning, fundraising, and managing nonprofit organizations.

*How to Apply For and Retain Exempt Status*. Publication 557, Internal Revenue Service. Available from local IRS offices.
Check local listings. This publication discusses how organizations become recognized as exempt from Federal Income Tax under Section 501A of the Internal Revenue Service code.

*In Art We Trust*, compiled and written by Robert W. Crawford. New York: Fedapt, 1981. Available from Foundation for the Extension and Development of the American Professional Theatre (Fedapt), 270 Lafayette Street, Suite 810, New York, NY 10012.
Manual that provides guidelines on the obligations, opportunities, and responsibilities for members of boards of trustees for not-for-profit performing arts institutions.

*No Quick Fix (Planning)*, Frederic W. Vogel. New York: Foundation for the Extension and Development of the American Professional Theatre. Available from Fedapt, 270 Lafayette Street, Suite 810, New York, NY 10012.
Handbook describing process and tools for nonprofit planning. (Prepared primarily for theater groups.)

*Philanthropy in the United States: History and Structure*, F. Emerson Andrews. New York: The Foundation Center, 1978. Available from The Foundation Center, 79 Fifth Avenue, New York, NY 10003.
A brief history of private foundations and philanthropy in the U.S., emphasizing structure and dimensions in the 1970s.

*Program Planning and Proposal Writing*, Norton J. Kiritz. Los Angeles: The Grantsmanship Center, 1980. Available from the Grantsmanship Center, 1015 West Olympic Boulevard, Los Angeles, CA 90015.
An extremely well-written and helpful guide to writing program proposals.

*The Proposal Writer's Swipe File*. Washington, DC: Taft Corporation, 1984. Available from Taft Corporation, 5125 MacArthur Boulevard, N.W., Washington, DC 20016.
Includes 15 proposals demonstrating various approaches, styles, and structures.

*Secrets of Major Gift Fund Raising*, Charles F. Mai. Washington, DC: The Taft Group, 1987. Available from The Taft Group, Public Service Materials Center, 5130 MacArthur Boulevard, N.W., Washington, DC 20016.
Do's and Don't's, cultivation of how to plan calls, ask for significant gifts and plan deferred giving programs from a veteran fundraiser with over 25 years of experience.

*Standards for Charitable Solicitation*, Helen O'Rourke. Arlington, VA: Council of Better Business Bureaus, annual. Available from Council of Better Business Bureaus Inc., 1515 Wilson Boulevard, Arlington, VA 22209.
A listing and explanation of standards of behavior for 501(c)(3) tax-exempt organizations that solicit funds from the public.

*The Successful Volunteer Organization*, Joan Flanagan. Chicago: Contemporary Books, 1982. Available from Contemporary Books, 180 North Michigan Avenue, Chicago, IL 60601.
A handbook providing practical advice for nonprofits on planning, fundraising, and management.

# Appendix B
# Keeping Up: Magazines, Newsletters, and Seminars

*Arts Management, The National News Service for Those Who Finance, Manage and Communicate the Arts*, Alvin H. Reiss, ed., five times a year. Available from Arts Management, 408 West 57th Street, New York, NY 10019.
Newsletter that covers reports on funding, awards, and updates on various arts news stories.

*Arts Reporting Service*, Charles Christopher Mark, ed., biweekly. Available from Arts Reporting Service, P.O. Box 40937, Washington, DC 20016.
Newsletter that reports on any interesting arts-related stories, job vacancies and changes, and federal funding issues.

*Business Week*, weekly. Available from McGraw-Hill Inc., 1221 Avenue of the Americas, New York, NY 10020.
Includes articles on businesses and corporate activities worldwide.

*Chronicle of Higher Education*, weekly. 1255 23rd Street, N.W., Washington, DC 20037.
Weekly newspaper featuring articles on philanthropy and fundraising including grant announcements for higher education programs.

*The Chronicle of Philanthropy*, bimonthly. Subscriptions available from P.O. Box 1989, Marion, OH 43305.
This bimonthly newspaper covers corporate and individual giving, foundations, fundraising, taxation, regulation and management.

*Donor Briefing*, biweekly. Available from Business Publishers, Inc., P.O. Box 5311, Evanston, IL 60204.
A compilation of grant information ranging from news related articles to a calendar of events and new publications available.

*Forbes Magazine*, biweekly. Available from Forbes Magazine Inc., 60 Fifth Avenue, New York, NY 10003.
Includes articles on corporate activities as well as in-depth reviews of the people involved.

*Fortune*, biweekly, Time, Inc. Available from Fortune Magazine Subscriptions, 541 North Fairbanks Court, Chicago, IL 60611.
A business publication that includes articles on corporate activities and profiles of businesses and their leaders.

*Foundation News*, bimonthly. Available from The Council of Foundations, Inc., 1828 L Street, N.W., Washington, DC 20036.
Features articles on grantmakers and grantmaking trends. Includes book reviews and classified advertisements.

*Fundraising Management*, monthly. Available from Hoke Communications, Inc. 224 Seventh Street, Garden City, NY 15530.
In-depth "How-To" articles on all aspects of fundraising.

*The Grantsmanship Center News*, bimonthly. Available from the Grantsmanship Center, 1031 South Grand Avenue, Los Angeles, CA 90015.
Information on both public and private sources of funding. Includes articles reviewing current issues in philanthropy as well as grant lists with deadlines and book reviews.

*The Non Profit Times*, monthly. Subscriptions available from P.O. Box 870, Wantagh, NY 11793-9817.
A monthly publication of non-profit news, marketing, and management.

*NSFRE Journal*, semiannual. Available from National Society for Fund-Raising Executives, Inc., Suite 1000, 1511 K Street, Washington, DC 20005.
Articles and reports on successful fundraising campaigns as well as advertisements of professional fundraisers.

*Voluntary Action Leadership*, quarterly. Available from Volunteer, the National Center, 1111 North 19th Street, Room 500, Arlington, VA 22209.
Articles, calendar of programs and courses, and book reviews of interest to volunteers.

# Appendix C
# Research Sources

## RESEARCHING PATRON SOURCES

*Fund Raiser's Guide to Private Fortunes.* Washington, DC: The Taft Group. Available from The Taft Group, Public Service Materials Center, 5130 MacArthur Boulevard, N.W., Washington, DC 20016.
A reference book devoted specifically to the research of major individual prospective donors.

*Martindale-Hubbell Law Directory,* 8 vols. Summit, NJ: Martindale-Hubbel, Inc. Available from Martindale-Hubbel, Inc., P.O. Box 1001, Summit, NJ 07901.
Complete legal directory service.

*Social Register.* New York: Social Register Association. Published yearly. Available from Social Register Association, 381 Park Avenue South, New York, NY 10016.
A record of names and addresses of prominent American families including information on clubs, births, marriages, and deaths.

*Wealth Holders of America.* San Francisco: Biodata. Updated annually. Available from Biodata Order Department, 358 Brannan St., San Francisco, CA 94107.
Indexed information about the assets and charitable and political contributions of America's millionaires.

*Who's Who in America.* Chicago: Marquis Who's Who, Inc. Published yearly. Available from Marquis Who's Who, Inc., 200 East Ohio Street, Chicago, IL 60611.
Other Marquis publications: *Who's Who in Finance and Industry, Who's Who in the East, Who's Who in the Midwest, Who's Who in the South and Southwest, Who's Who in the West, Who's Who of American Women.* Biographies profiling key men and women who influence the development of the United States, Canada, and Mexico, chronicling the lives and achievements of individuals whose contributions to society made them subjects of interest and inquiry.

## RESEARCHING BUSINESS SOURCES

*Annual Register of Grants Support.* Wilmette, IL: National Register
Publishing Co., 1985. Available from National Register Publishing
Co., 3004 Glenview Road, Wilmette, IL 60091.
Describes grant programs for research in all disciplines and subjects,
covering government, foundation, professional association, and special in-
terest group programs.

*Annual Survey of Corporate Contributions.* New York: The Conference
Board. Available from The Conference Board, 845 Third Avenue,
New York, NY 10022.
Annual report outlining corporate giving trends and statistics.

*Corporate 500: The Directory of Corporate Philanthropy.* San Francisco:
Public Management Institute, 1985. Available from Public Management Institute, 333 Hayes Street, San Francisco, CA 94102.
Outlines giving interests, application procedures, and eligibility requirements for corporate giving programs and foundations.

*The Corporate 1000: A Directory of Who Runs the Top 1000 U.S.
Corporations.* Washington, DC: Monitor Publishing Co. Available
from Monitor Publishing Co., 1301 Pennsylvania Avenue, NW,
Suite 3000, Washington, DC 20004.
Lists the chief officers, staff, and board members of 1000 U.S. corpora-
tions.

*Corporate Foundation Profiles.* New York: The Foundation Center.
Available from The Foundation Center, 79 Fifth Avenue, New
York, NY 10003.
Detailed analyses of major corporate foundations, indexed by subject
interest, type of support offered, and geographic location.

*Corporate Fund Raising Directory.* New York: Public Service Materials
Center, 1984. Available from Public Service Materials Center, 415
Lexington Avenue, New York, NY 10017.
Describes giving programs of over 600 corporations with multiple indexes.

*Corporate Giving Watch.* Washington, DC: The Taft Group. Published
monthly. Available from The Taft Group, 5130 MacArthur Boulevard, N.W., Washington, DC 20016.
Articles analyzing corporate philanthropy, including listing of recent corporate grants.

*Directory of Corporate Affiliations: Who Owns Whom, A Family Tree of
Every Corporate Organization in America.* Wilmette, IL: National
Register Publishing Co., Inc., annual. Available from National
Register Publishing Co., Inc., 5201 Old Orchard Road, Skokie, IL
60077.
A complex listing of corporate organizations in the U.S. and what other
companies they own or are connected with.

*Dun & Bradstreet Million Dollar Directory,* 5 vols. New York: Dun & Bradstreet, Inc, annual. Available from Dun's Marketing Services, One Penn Plaza, New York, NY 10019.
Profiles of over 160,000 of America's most productive companies both publicly and privately held.

*Dun & Bradstreet Reference Book of Corporate Management,* 4 vols. New York: Dun & Bradstreet, Inc., annual. Available from Dun & Bradstreet, Inc., 99 Church Street, New York, NY 10007.
Detailed biographical information on 200,000 corporate leaders from 12,000 of America's top companies.

*The Forbes 500 Annual Directory,* annual. Available from Forbes Magazine, Inc., 60 Fifth Avenue, New York, NY 10011.
The nation's largest companies ranked and listed by sales, profits, assets, and market value.

*The Fortune Directory of the 500 Largest Industrial Corporations,* annual. Available from Time Inc., 541 North Fairbanks Court, Chicago, IL 60611.
The largest industrial corporations in the U.S. ranked by 14 measures with profiles on the best and the worst and the economic trends of the past year.

*Guide to Corporate Giving,* Robert Porter, ed. New York: American Council for the Arts, 1987. Available from American Council for the Arts, 570 Seventh Avenue, New York, NY 10018.
Describes giving programs of over 700 U.S. corporations with emphasis on funding for the arts.

*Moody's Industrial Manual,* 2 vols. New York: Moody's Investors Services, Inc., annual. Available from Moody's Investors Services, Inc., 99 Church Street, New York, NY 10007.
Provides extensive historical and financial information on companies listed on the New York Stock Exchange as well as regional American exchanges. See also *Moody's Public Utility Manual.*

*National Directory of Corporate Public Affairs 1986.* Washington, DC: Columbia Books, Inc. Available from Columbia Books, 1350 New York Avenue, NW, Suite 207, Washington, DC 20005.
Provides a profile of the corporate public affairs profession in the United States including the identification of key people.

*O'Dwyer's Directory of Public Relations Firms,* annual. New York: J.R. O'Dwyer Co., Inc. Available from J.R. O'Dwyer Co., Inc., 271 Madison Avenue, New York, NY 10016.
Directory containing listings of more than 1,800 public relations firms and public relations departments of advertising agencies and their branches.

*Standard & Poor's Register of Corporations, Directors, Executives,* 3 vols. New York: Standard & Poor's, annual with quarterly updates. Available from Standard & Poor's, 25 Broadway, New York, NY 10004.
Listing of over 45,000 corporations with telephone numbers, officers,

directors, and key staff, principal business products and services, annual sales, and number of employees.

*Standard Directory of Advertising Agencies.* Wilmette, IL: National Register Publishing Co., Inc., annual with quarterly updates. Available from National Register Publishing Co., Inc., 3004 Glenview Road, Wilmette, IL 60091.
A comprehensive directory of U.S. and international ad agenices. Entries include name, address, year founded, number of employees, national association memberships, approximate annual billing, personnel, accounts, and the addresses and key personnel of branch offices.

*Taft Corporate Giving Directory.* Washington, DC: The Taft Corporation, published yearly. Available from The Taft Corporation, 5125 MacArthur Boulevard, N.W., Washington, DC 20016.
Directory of over 500 major corporate giving programs and company foundations.

## RESEARCHING FOUNDATION SOURCES

*America's Hidden Philanthropic Wealth.* Washington, DC: The Taft Group, 1988. Available from The Taft Group, Public Service Materials Center, 5130 MacArthur Boulevard, N.W., Washington, DC 20016.
Provides information on more than 300 of tomorrow's potential foundation giants. America's Newest Foundations, Washington, DC: The Taft Group. Available from The Taft Group, Public Service Materials Center, 5130 MacArthur Boulevard, N.W., Washington, DC 20016. Provides comprehensive coverage of over 300 grant-making foundations created since 1980.

*Comsearch Printouts: Geographic.* New York: The Foundation Center, annual. Available from The Foundation Center, 79 Fifth Avenue, New York, NY 10003.
A listing of grants awarded to organizations in specific geographic areas, arranged alphabetically by foundation name.

*Comsearch Printouts: Special Topics.* New York: The Foundation Center, annual. Available from The Foundation Center, 79 Fifth Avenue, New York, NY 10003.
A listing of grants by topics awarded to organizations in the fields of non-profit management, education, health care, welfare, and many others.

*Comsearch Printouts: Subjects.* New York: The Foundation Center, annual. Available from The Foundation Center, 79 Fifth Avenue, New York, NY 10003.
A listing of grants awarded in specific subject fields, arranged by foundation state and name.

*The Foundation Directory.* New York: The Foundation Center, annual. Available from The Foundation Center, 79 Fifth Avenue, New York, NY 10003.
Listing of private grantmaking foundations in the U.S. with assets of $1 million or more that award grants totalling at least $100,000 a year.

*Foundation Giving Watch.* Washington, DC: The Taft Group, monthly. Available from The Taft Group, 5130 MacArthur Boulevard, N.W., Washington, DC 20016.
Brief reports on foundation programs, giving trends, and recent grants.

*Foundation Grants Index Annual.* New York: The Foundation Center, annual. Available from The Foundation Center, 79 Fifth Avenue, New York, NY 10003.
A list of all grants reported in the previous year, indexed by name of recipient organizations as well as subject focus of each grant.

*National Data Book,* 2 vols. New York: The Foundation Center, annual. Available from The Foundation Center, 79 Fifth Avenue, New York, NY 10003.
The only directory currently published listing all active grantmaking foundations in the United States.

*People in Philanthropy.* Washington, DC: The Taft Corporation, 1988. Available from The Taft Corporation, 5125 MacArthur Boulevard, N.W., Washington, DC 20016.
A guide to philanthropic leaders, major donors, and funding connections, listing America's wealthiest philanthropists, foundation trustees, and corporate personalities.

*Source Book Profiles,* 2 vols. New York: The Foundation Center, annual. Available from The Foundation Center, 79 Fifth Avenue, New York, NY 10003.
List of the 1,000 top grantmakers in the United States, providing extensive descriptions of each foundation's giving program, application procedures, and giving history.

*Taft Foundation Reporter.* Washington, DC: The Taft Corporation, published yearly. Available from The Taft Corporation, 5125 MacArthur Boulevard, N.W., Washington, DC 20016.
Directory of 500 major private foundations, indexed by state, type of grant, field of interest, and directors.

*The Taft Trustees of Wealth: A Biographical Directory of Private Foundation and Corporate Foundation Officers.* Washington, DC: The Taft Corporation. Available from The Taft Corporation, 5125 MacArthur Boulevard, N.W., Washington, DC 20016.
A listing of current biographical information on individuals who manage the philanthropic activities of thousands of grant-making foundations. Last published in 1983. Function taken over in *People in Philanthropy.*

## RESEARCHING GOVERNMENT SOURCES

*The Catalog of Federal Domestic Assistance.* Washington, DC: U.S. Office of Management and Budget, annual with supplements. Available from Superintendent of Documents, U.S. Government Printing Office, Washington, DC 20402.
The essential guide to federal funding assistance available.

*Congressional Yellow Book.* Washington, DC: Monitor Publishing Co., updated quarterly. Available from Monitor Publishing Co., 1301 Pennsylvania Avenue, NW, Suite 3000, Washington, DC 20004.
A loose-leaf directory of members of Congress, their committees, and key aides.

*Federal Funding Guide.* Arlington, VA: Government Information Service, 1985. Available from Government Information Service.
A detailed guide to federal programs, highlighting statutory, regulatory, and budgetary changes, which provide assistance to all types of nonprofit organizations.

*Federal Register.* Washington, DC: U.S. Office of the Federal Register, daily. Available from Superintendent of Documents, U.S. Government Printing Office, Washington, DC 20402.
A directory of federal departments and agencies.

*Federal Yellow Book.* Washington, DC: Monitor Publishing Co, annual with updates. Available from Monitor Publishing Co., 1301 Pennsylvania Avenue, NW, Suite 3000, Washington, DC 20004.
Directory of federal departments and agencies.

*State Yellow Book.* Washington, DC: Monitor Publishing Co. Available Spring 1989 from Monitor Publishing Co., 1301 Pennsylvania Avenue, NW, Suite 3000, Washington, DC 20004.
A guidebook of state agencies.

*A Guide to the National Endowment for the Arts,* annual. Available from The National Endowment for the Arts, Nancy Hanks Center, 1100 Pennsylvania Avenue, NW, Washington, DC 20506.
A booklet designed to familiarize individuals and organizations with the Endowment. Describes purpose of programs and types of support available.

# Appendix D
# State Foundation Directories

## Alabama

*Alabama Foundation Directory.* Available from Reference Department, Birmingham Public Library, 2100 Park Place, Birmingham, AL 35203.

*Foundation Profiles of the Southeast: Alabama, Arkansas, Louisiana, Mississippi.* Available from James H. Taylor Associates, Inc., 804 Main Street, Williamsburg, KY 40769.

## Arkansas (*See also* Alabama)

*Guide to Arkansas Funding Sources.* Available from Independent Community Consultants, P.O. Box 1673, West Memphis, AR 72301.

## California

*Guide to California Foundations.* Available from Northern California Grantmakers, 334 Kearny Street, San Francisco, CA 94108.

*National Directory of Corporate Charity: California Edition.* Available from Regional Young Adult Project, 330 Ellis Street, Room 506, San Francisco, CA 94102.

*San Diego County Foundation Directory.* Available from San Diego Community Foundation, 625 Broadway, Suite 1015, San Diego, CA 92101.

*The Directory of the Major California Foundations.* Available from Logos Associates, 7 Park St., Rm. 212, Attleboro, MA 02703.

*Small Change from Big Bucks: A Report and Recommendations on Bay Area Foundations and Social Change.* Available from Regional Young Adult Project, 330 Ellis Street, Room 506, San Francisco, CA 94102.

*Where the Money's At, How to Reach Over 500 California Grant-Making Foundations.* Available from Irving R. Warner, 3235 Berry Drive, Studio City, CA 91604.

## Colorado

*Colorado Foundation Directory, 1986-1987*, 5th edition. Available from Colorado Foundation Directory, Junior League of Denver, Inc., 6300 East Yale Avenue, Denver, CO 80222.

## Connecticut

*Directory of the Major Connecticut Foundations.* Available from Logos, Inc., 7 Park Street, Room 212, Attleboro, MA 02703.

*1985-1986 Connecticut Foundation Directory.* Available from DATA, 880 Asylum Avenue, Hartford, CT 06103.

*1986-1987 Guide to Corporate Giving in Connecticut.* Available from DATA, 880 Asylum Avenue, Hartford, CT 06105.

## Delaware

*Delaware Foundations.* Available from United Way of Delaware, Inc., 701 Shipley Street, Wilmington, DE 19801.

## District of Columbia

*The Directory of Foundations of the Greater Washington Area.* Available from the Community Foundation of Greater Washington, 3221 M Street, N.W., Washington, DC 20007 or College University Research Institute, Inc., 1701 K Street, N.W., Washington, DC 20006.

## Florida

*The Complete Guide to Florida Foundations 1985/1986.* Available from Adams and Co., Inc., Publications Department, P.O. Box 561565, Miami, FL 33156.

*Foundations Profiles of the Southeast: Florida.* Available from James H. Taylor Associates, Inc., 804 Main Street, Williamsburg, KY 40769.

## Georgia

*Guide to Foundations in Georgia.* Available from Atlanta-Fulton Public Library, #1 Margaret Mitchell Square, Atlanta, GA 30303.

## Hawaii

*A Guide to Charitable Trusts and Foundations in the State of Hawaii.* Available from Alu Like, Inc., 401 Kamakee Street, 3rd Floor, Honolulu, HI 96814.

## Idaho

*Directory of Idaho Foundations, 1984.* Available from Caldwell Public Library, 1010 Dearborn, Caldwell, ID 83605.

## Illinois

*The Chicago Corporate Connection: A Directory of Chicago Area Corporate Contributors, Including Downstate Illinois and Northern Indiana.* Available from Donors Forum of Chicago, 208 South LaSalle Street, Chicago, IL 60604.

*Donors Forum Members Grants List 1984.* Available from Donors Forum of Chicago, 208 South LaSalle Street, Chicago, IL 60604.

*Illinois Foundation Directory.* Available from the Foundation Data Center, Kenmar Center, 401 Kenmar Circle, Minnetonka, MN 55343.

## Indiana

*Indiana Foundations: A Directory.* Available from Central Research Systems, 320 North Meridan, Suite 515, Indianapolis, IN 46204.

## Iowa

*Iowa Directory of Foundations.* Available from Trumpet Associates, Inc., P.O. Box 172, Dubuque, IA 52001.

## Kansas

*Directory of Kansas Foundations.* Available from Association of Community Arts Agencies of Kansas, P.O. Box 62, Oberlin, KS 67749.

## Kentucky

*Foundation Profiles of the Southeast: Kentucky, Tennessee, Virginia.* Available from James H. Taylor Associates, Inc., 804 Main Street, Williamsburg, KY 40769.

*A Guide to Kentucky Grantmakers.* Available from Louisville Community Foundation, Inc., Three Riverfront Plaza, Louisville, KY 40202.

## Louisiana (*See* Alabama)

## Maine

*A Directory of Foundations in the State of Maine.* Available from Center for Research and Advanced Study, University of Southern Maine, 246 Deering Avenue, Portland, ME 04102.

*Maine Corporate Funding Directory.* Available from the Center for Research and Advanced Study, University of Southern Maine, 246 Deering Avenue, Portland, ME 04102.

*Guide to Corporate Giving in Maine.* Available from OUA/DATA, 81 Saltonstall Avenue, New Haven, CT 06513.

## Maryland

*1984 Annual Index Foundation Reports.* Available from the Office of the Attorney General, 7 North Calvert Street, Baltimore, MD 21202.

## Massachusetts

*Massachusetts Grantmakers.* Available from Associated Grantmakers of Massachusetts, Inc., 294 Washington St., Suite 501, Boston, MA 02108.

*Directory of the Major Greater Boston Foundations.* Available from Logos Associates, 12 Gustin, Attleboro, MA 02703.

*Guide to Corporate Giving in Massachusetts.* Available from OUA/DATA, 81 Saltonstall Avenue, New Haven, CT 06513.

*Private Sector Giving: Greater Worcester Area.* Available from The Social Service Planning Corporation, 340 Main Street, Suite 329, Worcester, MA 01608.

## Michigan

*The Michigan Foundation Directory.* Available from Michigan League for Human Services, 300 North Washington Square, Suite 401, Lansing, MI 48933.

## Minnesota

*Minnesota Foundation Directory.* Available from Foundation Data Center, Kenmar Center, 401 Kenmar Circle, Minnetonka, MN 55343.

*Guide to Minnesota Foundations and Corporate Giving Programs.* Available from University of Minnesota Press, 2037 University Avenue S.E., Minneapolis, MN 55414.

## Mississippi (*See* Alabama)

## Missouri

*The Directory of Missouri Foundations.* Available from Swift Associates, P.O. Box 28033, St. Louis, MO 63119.

## Montana

*The Montana and Wyoming Foundations Directory.* Available from Grant Assistance, Eastern Montana College Library, 1500 North 30th Street, Billings, MT 59101.

## Nebraska

*Nebraska Foundation Directory.* Available from Junior League of Omaha, 808 South 74th Plaza, Omaha, NE 68114.

## Nevada

*Nevada Foundation Directory.* Available from Community Relations Department, Las Vegas–Clark County Library District, 1401 East Flamingo Road, Las Vegas, NV 89109.

## New Hampshire

*1984-1985 Guide to Corporate Giving in New Hampshire.* Available from OUA/DATA, 81 Saltonstall Avenue, New Haven, CT 06513.

*Directory of Charitable Funds in New Hampshire.* Available from the Division of Charitable Trusts, 400 State House Annex, Concord, NH 03301-6397.

## New Jersey

*The New Jersey Mitchell Guide: Foundations, Corporations, and Their Managers.* Available from The Mitchell Guide, P.O. Box 413, Princeton, NJ 08542.

*The Directory of the Major New Jersey Foundations.* Available from Logos Associates, Room 212, 7 Park Street, Attleboro, MA 02703.

## New Mexico

*New Mexico Private Foundations Directory.* Available from New Moon Consultants, P.O. Box 532, Tijeras, NM 87059.

## New York

*Guide to Grantmakers: Rochester Area.* Published by Reynolds Information Center, Monroe County Library System. May be used in libraries of Monroe County Library System.

*The Mitchell Guide to Foundations, Corporations and Their Managers: Central New York State* (includes Binghamton, Corning, Elmira, Geneva, Ithaca, Oswego, Syracuse and Utica). Available from The Mitchell Guide, P.O. Box 413, Princeton, NJ 08542.

*The Mitchell Guide to Foundations, Corporations and Their Managers: Long Island* (includes Nassau and Suffolk Counties). Available from The Mitchell Guide, P.O. Box 413, Princeton, NJ 08542.

*The Mitchell Guide to Foundations, Corporations and Their Managers: Upper Hudson Valley* (includes the Capital Area, Glenns Falls, Newburgh, Plattsburgh, Poughkeepsie and Schenectady). Available from The Mitchell Guide, P.O. Box 413, Princeton, NJ 08542.

*The Mitchell Guide to Foundations, Corporations and Their Managers: Westchester* (includes Putnam, Rockland and parts of Orange County). Available from The Mitchell Guide, P.O. Box 413, Princeton, NJ 08542.

*The Mitchell Guide to Foundations, Corporations and Their Managers: Western New York State* (includes Buffalo, Jamestown, Niagara Falls and Rochester). Available from The Mitchell Guide, P.O. Box 413, Princeton, NJ 08542.

*The New York City Mitchell Guide: Foundations, Corporations and Their Managers.* Available from The Mitchell Guide, P.O. Box 413, Princeton, NJ 08542.

## North Carolina

*Foundation Profiles of the Southeast: North Carolina, South Carolina.* Available from James H. Taylor Associates, Inc., 804 Main Street, Williamsburg, KY 70769.

*Grantseeking in North Carolina: A Guide to Foundation and Corporate Giving.* Available from North Carolina Center for Public Policy Research, P.O. Box 430, Raleigh, NC 27602.

## Ohio

*Charitable Foundations Directory of Ohio.* Available from Charitable Foundations Directory, Attention: Faye Sebert, Attorney General Celebrezze's Office, 30 East Broad Street, 15th Floor, Columbus, OH 43215.

*Guide to Charitable Foundations in the Greater Akron Area.* Available from Grants Department, United Way of Summit County, P.O. Box 1260, 90 North Prospect Street, Akron, OH 44304.

*Directory of Dayton Area Grantmakers.* Available from Belinda Hogue, 449 Patterson Road, Apt. A, Dayton, OH 45419.

*The Source: A Directory of Cincinnati Foundations.* Available from the Junior League of Cincinnati, Grantsmanship Committee, Regency Square, 2334 Dana Avenue, Cincinnati, OH 45208.

## Oklahoma

*Directory of Oklahoma Foundations.* Available from University of Oklahoma Press, 1005 Asp Avenue, Norman, OK 73019.

## Oregon

*The Guide to Oregon Foundations.* Available from Bonnie Smith, the United Way of the Columbia-Willamette, 718 West Burnside, Portland, OR 97209.

## Pennsylvania

*Directory of Pennsylvania Foundations.* Available from Directory of Pennsylvania Foundations, P.O. Box 336, Springfield, PA 19064.

## Rhode Island

*Directory of Grant-Making Foundations in Rhode Island.* Available from the Council for Community Services, 229 Waterman Street, Providence, RI 02906.

*Guide to Corporate Giving in Rhode Island.* Available from OUA/DATA, 81 Saltonstall Avenue, New Haven, CT 06513.

## South Carolina (*See also* North Carolina)

*South Carolina Foundation Directory.* Out of print. Available on inter-library loan from South Carolina State Library, Columbia, SC.

## Tennessee (*See also* Kentucky)

*Tennessee Directory of Foundations and Corporate Philanthropy.* Available from Executive Management Services, Room 508, City Hall, 125 North Mid-America Mall, Memphis, TN 38103.

## Texas

*The Hooper Directory of Texas Foundations.* Available from Funding Information Center of Texas, 507 Brooklyn, San Antonio, TX 78215.

*Directory of Dallas County Foundations.* Available from Urban Information Center, Dallas Public Library, 1515 Young St., Dallas, TX 75201.

*Directory of Tarrant County Foundations.* Available from Funding Information Center, Texas Christian University Library, P.O. Box 32904, Fort Worth, TX 76129.

## Utah

*A Directory of Foundations in Utah.* Available from University of Utah Press, 101 University Services Building, Salt Lake City, UT 84112.

*The Directory of Utah Foundations.* Available from MG Enterprises, 839 East South Temple #107, Salt Lake City, UT 84102.

## Vermont

*OUA/DATA's 1984-1985 Guide to Corporate and Foundation Giving in Vermont.* Available from OUA/DATA, 81 Saltonstall Avenue, New Haven, CT 06513.

## Virginia (*See also* Kentucky)

*Virginia Foundations 1985.* Available from Sharen Sinclair, Grants Resources Library, Hampton City Hall, 9th Floor, 22 Lincoln Street, Hampton, VA 23669.

## Washington

*Charitable Trust Directory.* Available from the Office of the Attorney General, Temple of Justice, Olympia, WA 98504.

## Wisconsin

*Foundations in Wisconsin: A Directory 1984.* Available from The Foundation Collection, Marquette University Memorial Library, 1415 West Wisconsin Avenue, Milwaukee, WI 53233.

## Wyoming (*See also* Montana)

*Wyoming Foundations Directory.* Available from Laramie County Community College Library, 1400 East College Drive, Cheyenne, WY 82007.

# Appendix E
# State Arts Councils

**Alabama State Council on the Arts &
Humanities**
1 Dexter Avenue
Montgomery, AL 36130-5401
(205) 261-4076

**Alaska State Council on the Arts**
619 Warehouse Avenue, Suite 220
Anchorage, AK 99501
(907) 279-1558

**American Samoa Council on Culture,
Art and Humanities**
P.O. Box 1540
Office of the Governor
Pago Pago, AS 96799
(011) 684-633-4347

**Arizona Commission on the Arts**
417 West Roosevelt Avenue
Phoenix, AZ 85003
(602) 255-5882

**Arkansas Arts Council**
Heritage Center, Suite 200
225 E. Markham
Little Rock, AR 72201
(501) 371-2539

**California Arts Council**
1901 Broadway, Suite A
Sacramento, CA 95818
(916) 322-8911

**Colorado Council on the Arts &
Humanities**
770 Pennsylvania Street
Denver, CO 80203
(303) 866-2617

**Connecticut Commission on the Arts**
190 Trumbull Street
Hartford, CT 06103
(203) 566-4770

**Delaware State Arts Council**
820 North French Street
Wilmington, DE 19801
(302) 571-3540

**District of Columbia (DC)
Commission on the Arts**
1111 E Street, NW, Suite B500
Washington, DC 20005
(202) 724-5613

**Florida Arts Council**
Department of State, The Capitol
Tallahassee, FL 32301
(904) 487-2980

**Georgia Council for the Arts &
Humanities**
2082 East Exchange Place, Suite 100
Tucker, GA 30084
(404) 493-5780

**Guam Council on the Arts &
Humanities Agency**
Office of the Governor
P.O. Box 2950
Agana, GU 96910
(011) 671-477-7413

**State Foundation on Culture and the
Arts (Hawaii)**
335 Merchant Street, Suite 202
Honolulu, HI 96813
(808) 548-4145

**Idaho Commission on the Arts**
304 West State Street
Boise, ID 83720
(208) 334-2119

**Illinois Arts Council**
State of Illinois Center
100 W. Randolph Street, Suite
    10-500
Chicago, IL 60601
(312) 917-6750

**Indiana Arts Commission**
47 S. Pennsylvania Street, 6th Floor
Indianapolis, IN 46204
(317) 232-1268

**Iowa Arts Council**
State Capital Complex
1223 East Court Avenue
Des Moines, IA 50319
(515) 281-4451

**Kansas Arts Commission**
Jayhawk Tower
700 Jackson
Suite 1004
Topeka, KS 66603
(913) 296-3335

**Kentucky Arts Council**
Berry Hill
Frankfort, KY 40601
(502) 564-3757

**Louisiana State Arts Council**
666 N. Foster Drive
P.O. Box 44247
Baton Rouge, LA 70804
(504) 342-8180

**Maine Arts Commission**
55 Capitol Street
State House Station 25
Augusta, ME 04333
(207) 289-2724

**Maryland State Arts Council**
15 West Mulberry Street
Baltimore, MD 21201
(301) 685-6740

**Massachusetts Council on the Arts &**
    **Humanities**
80 Boylston Street, 10th Floor
Boston, MA 02116
(617) 727-3668

**Michigan Council for the Arts**
1200 6th Avenue, Executive Plaza
Detroit, MI 48226
(313) 256-3735

**Minnesota State Arts Board**
432 Summit Avenue
St. Paul, MN 55102
(612) 297-2603

**Mississippi Arts Commission**
301 North Lamar Street
suite 400
Jackson, MS 39201
(601) 354-7336

**Missouri Arts Council**
111 North 7th Street, Suite 105
St. Louis, MO 63101
(314) 444-6845

**Montana Arts Council**
48 North Last Chance Gulch
Helena, MT 59620
(406) 443-4339

**Nebraska Arts Council**
1313 Farnam-on-the-Mall
Omaha, NE 68102
(402) 554-2122

**Nevada State Council on the Arts**
329 Flint Street
Reno, NV 89501
(702) 789-0225

**New Hampshire State Council on the**
    **Arts**
Phenix Hall
40 North Main Street
Concord, NH 03301
(603) 271-2789

**New Jersey State Council on the**
    **Arts**
109 West State Street
Trenton, NJ 08625
(609) 292-6130

**New Mexico Arts Division**
224 East Palace Avenue
Santa Fe, NM 87501
(505) 827-6490

**New York State Council on the Arts**
915 Broadway
New York, NY 10010
(212) 614-2909

**North Carolina Arts Council**
Department of Cultural Resources
Raleigh, NC 27611
(919) 733-2821

**North Dakota Council on the Arts**
Black Building, Suite 606
Fargo, ND 58102
(701) 237-8962

**Commonwealth Council for Arts and Culture (Northern Marianas Islands)**
P.O. Box 553, CHRB
Saipan, CM 96950
(011) 670-322-9982, 9983, FAX 9028

**Ohio Arts Council**
727 East Main Street
Columbus, OH 43205
(614) 466-2613

**State Arts Council of Oklahoma**
Jim Thorpe Building, #640
Oklahoma, OK 73105
(405) 521-2931

**Oregon Arts Commission**
835 Summer Street, NE
Salem, OR 97301
(503) 378-3625

**Pennsylvania Council on the Arts**
216 Finance Building
Harrisburg, PA 17120
(717) 787-6883

**Institute of Puerto Rican Culture**
P.O. Box 4184
San Juan, PR 00905
(809) 724-3210

**Rhode Island State Council on the Arts**
95 Cedar Street
Suite 103
Providence, RI 02903-4494
(401) 277-3880

**South Carolina Arts Commission**
1800 Gervais Street
Columbia, SC 29201
(803) 734-8696

**South Dakota Arts Council**
108 West 11th Street
Sioux Falls, SD 57102
(605) 399-6646

**Tennessee Arts Commission**
320 6th Avenue, North, Suite 100
Nashville, TN 37219
(615) 741-1701

**Texas Commission on the Arts**
P.O. Box 13406, Capitol Station
Austin, TX 78711
(512) 463-5535

**Utah Arts Council**
617 E. South Temple Street
Salt Lake City, UT 84102
(801) 533-5895

**Vermont Council on the Arts**
136 State Street
Montpelier, VT 05602
(802) 828-3291

**Virgin Islands Council on the Arts**
P.O. Box 103
St. Thomas, VI 00801
(809) 774-5984

**Virginia Commission for the Arts**
James Monroe Building
101 No. 14th Street, 17th Floor
Richmond, VA 23219
(804) 225-3132

**Washington State Arts Commission**
Mail Stop GH-1
Olympia, WA 98504
(206) 753-3860

**West Virginia Arts & Humanities Division**
Dept. of Culture & History
Capitol Complex
Charleston, WV 25305
(304) 348-0240

**Wisconsin Arts Board**
131 West Wilson Street
Suite 301
Madison, WI 53702
(608) 266-0190

**Wyoming Council on the Arts**
2320 Capitol Avenue
Cheyenne, WY 82002
(307) 777- 7742

# Appendix F
# State Humanities Councils

**Alabama Humanities Foundation**
Leslie Wright Fine Arts Center
Box 2280
Samford University
Birmingham, AL 35229
(205) 870-2300

**Alaska Humanities Forum**
430 West Seventh Avenue
Anchorage, AK 99501
(907) 272-5341

**Arizona Humanities Council**
2828 North Central, Suite 1111
Phoenix, AZ 85004
(602) 257-0335

**Arkansas Endowment for the
    Humanities**
The Remmel Building, Suite 102
1010 West 3rd Street
Little Rock, AR 72201
(501) 372-2672

**California Council for the Humanities**
312 Sutter Street, Suite 601
San Francisco, CA 94108
(415) 391-1474

**Colorado Endowment for the
    Humanities**
1836 Blake Street #100
Denver, CO 80202
(303) 292-4458

**Connecticut Humanities Council**
41 Lawn Avenue
Wesleyan Station
Middletown, CT 06457
(203) 347-6888

**Delaware Humanities Forum**
2600 Pennsylvania Avenue
Wilmington, DE 19806
(302) 573-4410

**D.C. Community Humanities Council**
1331 H Street, N.W.
Suite 310
Washington, DC 20005
202) 347-1732

**Florida Endowment for the
    Humanities**
P.O. Box 16989
University of South Florida
Tampa, FL 33687-6989
(813) 974-4094

**Georgia Endowment for the
    Humanities**
1589 Clifton Road, NE
Emory University
Atlanta, GA 30322
(404) 727-7500

**Hawaii Committee for the
    Humanities**
First Hawaiian Bank Building
3599 Waialae Avenue, Room 23
Honolulu, HI 96816
(808) 732-5402

**Idaho Humanities Council**
Room 300, Len B. Jordan Building
650 West State Street
Boise, ID 83720
(208) 345-5346

**Illinois Humanities Council**
618 South Michigan Avenue
Chicago, IL 60605
(312) 939-5212

**Indiana Committee for the
   Humanities**
1500 North Delaware Street
Indianapolis, IN 46202
(317) 638-1500

**Iowa Humanities Board**
Oakdale Campus
University of Iowa
N210 OH
Iowa City, IA 52242
(319) 353-6754

**Kansas Committee for the
   Humanities**
112 West Sixth Street, Suite 210
Topeka, KS 66603
(913) 357-0359

**Kentucky Humanities Council, Inc.**
417 Clifton Avenue
University of Kentucky
Lexington, KY 40506-0414
(606) 257-5932

**Louisiana Endowment for the
   Humanities**
1001 Howard Avenue, Suite 4407
New Orleans, LA 70013
(504) 523-4352

**Maine Humanities Council**
P.O. Box 7202
Portland, ME 04112
(207) 773-5051

**Maryland Humanities Council**
516 North Charles Street, #201
Baltimore, MD 21201
(301) 625-4830

**Massachusetts Foundation for the
   Humanities and Public Policy**
One Woodbridge Street
South Hadley, MA 01075
(413) 536-1385

**Michigan Council for the Humanities**
Nisbet Building, Suite 30
1407 South Harrison Road
East Lansing, MI 48824
(517) 355-0160

**Minnesota Humanities Commission**
580 Park Square Court
Sixth and Sibley Streets
St. Paul, MN 55101
(612) 224-5739

**Mississippi Committee for the
   Humanities**
3825 Ridgewood Road, Room 111
Jackson, MS 39211
(601) 9820-6752

**Missouri Humanities Council**
Lindell Blvd., Suite 210
St. Louis, MO 63108
(314) 531-1254

**Montana Committee for the
   Humanities**
P.O. Box 8036
Hellgate Station
Missoula, MT 59807
(406) 243-6022

**Nebraska Committee for the
   Humanities**
Suite 422 Lincoln Center Building
215 Centennial Mall South
Lincoln, NE 68508
(402) 474-2131

**Nevada Humanities Committee**
P.O. Box 8029
Reno, NV 89507
(702) 784-6587

**New Hampshire Council for the
   Humanities**
The Walker Building
15 South Fruit Street
Concord, NH 03301
(603) 224-4071

**New Jersey Committee for the
   Humanities**
73 Easton Avenue
New Brunswick, NJ 08901
(201) 932-7726

**New Mexico Endowment for the
   Humanities**
Onate Hall, Room 209
University of New Mexico
Albuquerque, NM 87131
(505) 277-3705

**New York Council for the Humanities**
198 Broadway, 10th Floor
New York, NY 10038
(212) 233-1131

**North Carolina Humanities Committee**
112 Foust Building,
    UNC-Greensboro
Greensboro, NC 27412
(919) 663-1948

**The Ohio Humanities Council**
760 Pleasant Ridge Avenue
Columbus, OH 43209
(612) 231-6879

**Oklahoma Foundation for the Humanities**
Executive Terrace Building
2809 Northwest Expressway—Suite 500
Oklahoma City, OK 73112
(405) 840-1721

**Oregon Committee for the Humanities**
418 S.W. Washington, Room 410
Portland, OR 97204
(503) 241-0543

**Pennsylvania Humanities Council**
401 North Broad Street
Philadelphia, PA 19108
(215) 925-1005

**Fundacion Puertorriquena de las Humanidades**
Box S-4307
Old San Juan, PR 00904
(809) 721-2087

**Rhode Island Committee for the Humanities**
463 Broadway
Providence, RI 02909
(401) 273-2250

**South Carolina Committee for the Humanities**
P.O. Box 6925
Columbia, SC 29260
(803) 738-1850

**South Dakota Committee on the Humanities**
Box 7050, University Station
Brookings, SD 57007
(605) 688-6113

**Tennessee Humanities Council**
1003 18th Avenue South
Nashville, TN 37212
(615) 320-7001

**Texas Committee for the Humanities**
1604 Nueces
Austin, TX 78701
(512) 473-8585

**Utah Endowment for the Humanities**
Grant House, P.O. Box 58
Hyde Park, VT 05655
(802) 888-3183

**Virginia Islands Humanities Council**
Market Square—Conrad Building
#6 Torvet Straede/Fourth Floor—Suite #6
P.O. Box 1829
St. Thomas, VI 00801
(809) 776-4044

**Washington Commission for the Humanities**
Lowman Building, Suite 312
107 Cherry Street
Seattle, WA 98104
(206) 682-1770

**Humanities Foundation of West Virginia**
Box 204
Institute, WV 25112
(304) 768-8869

**Wisconsin Humanities Council**
716 Langdon Street
Madison, WI 53706
(608) 262-0706

**Wyoming Council for the Humanities**
Box 3972—University Station
Laramie, WY 82071-3972
(307) 766-6496

# Appendix G
# Fundraising and Management Organizations

**Accountants for the Public Interest**
Support Center of New York
36 West 44th Street
Room 1208
New York, NY 10036
(212) 302-6940

**The Advertising Council**
825 Third Avenue
New York, NY 10022

**American Association of
    Fund-Raising Counsel, Inc.**
25 W. 43 Street
New York, NY 10036

**American Council on Education**
One Dupont Circle, NW
Washington, DC 20036

**American Management Association
    (AMA)**
135 W. 50th Street
New York, NY 10020

**Association of American Colleges**
1818 R Street, NW
Washington, DC 20009

**Association for Volunteer
    Administration (AVA)**
P.O. Box 4584
Boulder, CO 80306

**Committee for Economic
    Development**
477 Madison Avenue
New York, NY 10022

**The Conference Board**
845 Third Avenue
New York, NY 1022

**Council for Advancement and Support
    of Education**
11 Dupont Circle, NW
Washington, DC 20036

**Council for Financial Aid to
    Education, Inc.**
680 Fifth Avenue
New York, NY 10019

**Council of Better Business Bureaus,
    Inc.**
1515 Wilson Blvd.
Arlington, VA 22209

**Council on Foundations, Inc.**
1828 L Street, NW
Washington, DC 20036

**Council of State Governments**
270 Broadway
New York, NY 10007

**Direct Mail Fundraisers Association**
810 Seventh Avenue
New York, NY 10019

**The Foundation Center**
79 Fifth Avenue
New York, NY 10019

**Fund Raising Institute**
Box 365
Ambler, PA 19002

**The Grantsmanship Center**
1015 West Olympic Boulevard
Los Angeles, CA 90015

**Independent Sector**
1828 L Street, NW
Washington, DC 20036

**Independent College Funds of America, Inc.**
4 Landmark Square, S-218
Stamford, CT 06901-2502

**National Association of Independent Colleges and Universities**
122 C Street, NW
Washington, DC 20007

**National Association of Independent Schools Inc.**
18 Tremont Street
Boston, MA 02109

**National Center for Charitable Statistics**
1828 L Street, NW
Washington, DC 20036

**National Charities Information Bureau**
19 Union Square West
New York, NY 10003

**National Committee for Responsive Philanthropy**
2001 S Street, NW
Washington, DC 20009

**National Society of Fund Raising Executives**
1101 King Street, Suite 3000
Alexandria, VA 22314

**Nonprofit Coordinating Committee of New York**
419 Park Avenue South
16th Floor
New York, NY 10016
(212) 689-1240

**Program on Non-Profit Organizations at Yale University (PONPO)**
P.O. Box 154, Yale Station
88 Trumbull Street
New Haven, CT 06520

**Public Management Institute**
348 Brannan Street
San Francisco, CA 94107

**Volunteer: The National Center**
1111 North 19 Street
Arlington, VA 22209

# Appendix H
# Arts and Cultural Organizations

**American Association of Museums**
1055 Thomas Jefferson Street, NW
Washington, DC 20034

**American Arts Alliance**
1319 F Street, NW
Suite 307
Washington, DC 20004
(202) 737-1727

**American Council for the Arts**
1285 Avenue of the Americas
Floor 3, Area M
New York, NY 10019

**American Film Institute**
The John F. Kennedy Center for the
    Performing Arts
Washington, DC 20566

**American Symphony Orchestra
    League**
633 E Street, NW
Washington, DC 20004

**Arts & Business Council Inc.**
130 East 40th Street
New York, NY 10016

**ARTS International**
Institute of International Education
809 UN Plaza
New York, NY 10017
(212) 984-5370

**Association of Hispanic Arts (AHA)**
200 E. 87th Street
New York, NY 10028

**Association of Independent Video and
    Filmmakers**
625 Broadway
New York, NY 10012

**Association of Performing Arts
    Presentors**
Suite 620
1112 16th St., NW
Washington, DC 20036
(202) 833-2787

**Business Committee for the Arts**
1775 Broadway
New York, NY 10019

**Center for Arts Information**
625 Broadway
New York, NY 10012

**Chamber Music America**
1372 Broadway
New York, NY 10018

**Dance USA**
633 E Street, NW
Washington, DC 20001

**Foundation for the Extension and
    Development of the American
    Professional Theatre (FEDAPT)**
270 Lafayette St.
New York, NY 10012
(212) 966-9344

**Institute for Museum Services**
1100 Pennsylvania Avenue, NW
Washington, DC 20506

**Meet the Composer**
2112 Broadway
New York, NY 10023
(212) 787-3601

**National Assembly of Local Arts
    Agencies**
1625 I Street, NW
Washington, DC 20006

**National Assembly of State Arts
    Agencies (NASAA)**
1010 Vermont Avenue, NW
Washington, DC 20005

**National Endowment for the Arts**
1100 Pennsylvania Avenue, NW
Washington, DC 20506

**National Endowment for the
    Humanities**
1100 Pennsylvania Avenue, NW
Washington, DC 20506

**Opera America, Inc.**
633 E Street, NW
Washington, DC 20004

**Poets & Writers, Inc.**
201 West 54th Street
New York, NY 10019

**Theatre Communications Group**
355 Lexington Avenue
New York, NY 10017

**Volunteer Lawyers for the Arts
    (VLA)**
1560 Broadway, Suite 711
New York, NY 10036

# Appendix I: Examples of Fundraising Documents

## ANNUAL REPORT—President's Letter

The Annual Report of an institution chronicles its program activities and financial status during a complete fiscal year.

    The Annual Report featured here included a letter from the President, a list of performance events, narratives and photographs relating to each major program initiative, a donor listing, and a financial summary based on the institution's audit. The cover displayed a photograph of a performance highlight from the past year.

This Annual Report is a record of the 125th season of the Brooklyn Academy of Music. It was a celebration of the Academy's glorious history and its continuing vigor.

Two special events had particular significance, one a celebration of Brooklyn-born George Gershwin (who died 50 years ago) and his brother Ira; the second being an exposition of the different cultures that coexist in Brooklyn today, called, BROOKLYN BRIDGES THE WORLD.

The Gershwin celebration was of a special character. A tremendous amount of work, scholarship, organization, creation, and production went into the one-night GERSHWIN GALA, which BAM produced in collaboration with WNET ("Great Performances"), and B.B.C. television. And the same effort went into the concert versions, performed together in one evening, of the Gershwins' OF THEE I SING and LET 'EM EAT CAKE. The heroes of these two events are too numerous to mention here; they include researchers, orchestrators, conceivers, conductors, producers, directors, choreographers, designers, stage performers, musicians, stage managers and all the staff and crews, front and backstage. Particularly, I want to thank the entire Gershwin family, especially Lenore Gershwin, Ira Gershwin's widow, and also I want to tip my hat to Maestro Michael Tilson Thomas, whose energy was prodigious and for making it possible for millions to enjoy the event on television. And we are grateful to CBS Records and Joe Dash for recording the two musicals for public release. It was a proud accomplishment for all concerned.

BROOKLYN BRIDGES THE WORLD was a showcase of Brooklyn talent and performing arts, an exposition of the varieties of American urban culture today. My thanks to Burl Hash and Taras Shipowick for shepherding this monumental project through its many difficult phases, and finally to exciting realization.

This past year also happened to be my 20th year at BAM, and I was happy to celebrate that anniversary with artists from my first years here: Merce Cunningham and John Cage opening our season and the NEXT WAVE Festival with their glorious ROARATORIO; Robert Wilson's and Philip Glass's stunning Rome Section of the CIVIL warS to close the Festival and Twyla Tharp with a spectacular four-week season in February.

Finally, and sadly, we all mourn two young men who contributed so much to BAM: Leonard Nutman, our Director of Operations, who was beloved by all of us; and Willi Smith, a wonderful, creative spirit.

Harvey Lichtenstein
President and Executive Producer

Photo 3 · 1987 by Bob Kramvrath

(Courtesy of The Brooklyn Academy of Music)

# ANNUAL REPORT—Program Listing

---

THE ENCHANTED TOY SHOP
Ballet America Concert Dancers
*January 5–9*

THE GREAT VAUDEVILLE
MAGIC SHOW
Landis & Co.
*January 12–16*

FAIR MEANS OR FOUL
After Dinner Opera Co.
*January 13 & 14*

DINOSAURS FOREVER
Michele Valeri
*January 12–23*

CALABASH AFRICAN
DANCE COMPANY
*January 20–23*

WHEN THE COOKIE
CRUMBLES, YOU CAN STILL
PICK UP THE PIECES
Theatreworks U.S.A.
*January 20–23*

MUSIC AND THE
UNDERGROUND RAILROAD
VNI
*January 28–30*

THE SILLY JELLYFISH
& ONIROKU
Hudson Vagabond Puppets
*February 9–12*

JUXTA-POSITIONS—
MOVEMENT THEATRE
Kuperberg Morris
*February 17–20*

THE EMPEROR'S
NEW CLOTHES
Theatreworks U.S.A.
*February 23–27*

SHERLOCK HOLMES AND
THE RED-HEADED LEAGUE
Theatreworks U.S.A.
*March 3–6*

SPANISH FOLKTALES
AND SONGS
Puerto Rico—Felix Pitre
*February 23–27*

OSCAR BRAND—
FROM THE REVOLUTION TO
THE ROLLING STONES
VNI
*March 17–20*

THE POTATO PEOPLE
Theatre Beyond Words
Ontario, Canada
*March 23–April 3*

THE FROG BRIDE &
OTHER TALES
The Shoestring Players
*April 22–24*

THE LITTLE PRINCE
Centro Teatro Ragazzi, Verona,
Italy
*April 27–May 1*

LA TROUPE CIRCUS
Montreal Canada
*May 11–May 15*

PETER & THE WOLF/
BREMENTOWN MUSICIANS
Hudson Vagabond Puppets
*May 18–22*

JUST SO STORIES
Mermaid Theatre, Nova Scotia,
Canada
*May 18–22*

YANKEE DOODLE DANDY
United States
*May 26–29*

SNOW WHITE AND THE
SEVEN DWARVES
Gingerbread Players & Jack
*June 1–12*

SPOLETO COMES TO BAM

---

GIAN CARLO MENOTTI,
*composer*
MARVIS MARTIN, *soprano*
KATHERINE CIESINSKI,
*mezzo-soprano*
DAVID GORDON, *tenor*
RAIMON BOLIPATA, *cello*
CARTER BREY, *cello*
NANCY ALLEN, *harp*
JEAN-YVES THIBAUDET, *piano*
CHARLES WADSWORTH, *piano*
RIDGE STRING QUARTET
*December 13*

JAIME LAREDO, *violin*
JEAN-YVES THIBAUDET *piano*
RIDGE QUARTET
*January 17*

YEFIM BRONFMAN, *piano*
MELIORA STRING QUARTET
*February 7*

EMERSON STRING QUARTET
SCOTT NICKRENZ, *viola*
COLIN CARR, *cello*
*February 28*

PAULA ROBISON, *flute*
FRANK MORELLI, *bassoon*
(11 winds, cello, and double bass)
*March 21*

PAULA ROBISON, *flute*
DOUGLAS BOYD, *oboe*
FRANK MORELLI, *bassoon*
KENNETH COOPER, *harpsichord*
WENDY YOUNG, *harpsichord*
*April 18*

JOSEPH SWENSEN, *violin*
SCOTT NICKRENZ, *viola*
CARTER BREY, *cello*
KATHRYN SELBY, *piano*
*May 2*

5

# ANNUAL REPORT—Description of Major Programs

She has choreographed for film *(Amadeus, White Nights)*, and created for Broadway *(Singin' in the Rain, The Catherine Wheel)*. She polarizes critics and sends audiences into euphoric frenzies. But no matter what she does, Twyla Tharp always leaves her own unique and indelible creative stamp on her work.

Nearly twenty years ago, the Brooklyn Academy of Music and Ms. Tharp first got together. Thus it was fitting that for its 125th Anniversary, BAM's Opera House should have been the setting for the first four-week season in New York of Twyla Tharp Dance, a season which broke all previous BAM box office records.

Nor was record-breaking attendance the season's only mark of success. Once again the energetic and unpredictable Ms. Tharp showed her ample creative genius in three programs which included the premieres of two amazing and diametrically different works: *In the Upper Room*, to a commissioned score by Philip Glass, and *Ballare* to music of Mozart.

Ms. Tharp's return to BAM marked her first New York season in over three years. She brought with her a new company and, in addition to the two premieres, five other dances from her amazing repertory of over eighty works.

The Tharp company's opening-night gala benefit on February 3, with Robert Redford as chairman, began with

what has become a Tharp classic, *Nine Sinatra Songs*. The program climaxed with the New York premiere of *In the Upper Room*, a work of such unrelenting energy that it literally left the audience, as well as the dancers, exhausted and exhilarated. The following night, Ms. Tharp's company presented their first performance of *As Time Goes By*, a work Ms. Tharp originally created for the Joffrey Ballet, plus a new production of *The Catherine Wheel* with a musical score by David Byrne. The third program, headlined by the premiere of *Ballare*, included *Fugue* and *Nine Sinatra Songs*. Ms. Tharp also revived her delightful *Baker's Dozen*, which was paired with *In the Upper Room* for the subscription performances following the opening night Gala.

BAM's Twyla Tharp Dance program was sponsored by grants from the Chase Manhattan Bank, N.A.; the Coca-Cola Foundation; Starrett City; and S. J. Conway & Company Inc.

*Opposite page: (Clockwise from top left)* Twyla Tharp Dance members Kevin Santee and Stephanie Foster in *Ballare;* John Carrafa and Sara Rudner in *Nine Sinatra Songs,* photos by Richard Avedon; Jennifer Way and Shelley Washington in *The Catherine Wheel,* photo by Herbert Migdoll; Shelley Washington and John Carrafa in *Baker's Dozen,* photo by Jack Mitchell. *Above:* Shelley Washington, Jamie Bishton, John Carrafa and Kevin O'Day performing *In the Upper Room,* photo by Herbert Migdoll.

# ANNUAL REPORT—Donor List

BAM DONORS

Brooklyn Academy of Music is owned by the City of New York and administered by the Brooklyn Academy of Music, Inc. BAM's operation is supported, in part, with public funds provided through the New York City Department of Cultural Affairs and with grants from the National Endowment for the Arts and the New York State Council on the Arts.

BAM wishes to thank the following individuals, foundations and corporations that support BAM's General Operating, NEXT WAVE, Challenge and Benefit Campaigns.

**LEADERSHIP**
Abraham & Straus/Federated Department Stores, Inc.
Anonymous
AT&T Foundation
The Vincent Astor Foundation
Bankers Trust Company
Brooklyn Union Gas Company
Louis Calder Foundation
Mary Flagler Cary Charitable Trust
Chase Manhattan Bank
Chemical Bank
Citibank, N.A.
Robert Sterling Clark Foundation, Inc.
Coca Cola Foundation
Columbia Pictures Industries
Con Edison
S. J. Conway & Company, Inc.
Educational Foundation of America
Eleanor Naylor Dana Charitable Trust
Delmar Management Corporation
The Aaron Diamond Foundation
Asher Edelman
Exxon Corporation
The Ford Foundation
Howard Gilman Foundation
Herman Goldman Foundation
The Greenwall Foundation
The William & Flora Hewlett Foundation
Mr. & Mrs. Sidney Kantor
J.M. Kaplan Fund, Inc.
Mr. & Mrs. Arthur J. Levitt Jr.
Sydney & Frances Lewis
Manufacturers Hanover Trust Company
Morgan Guaranty Trust Company
National Endowment for the Arts
National Westminster Bank USA
New York City Department of Cultural Affairs
New York Community Trust
New York State Council on the Arts
New York Telephone Company

The New York Times Company Foundation
The Pew Charitable Trusts
Philip Morris Companies Inc.
The Reed Foundation
Samuel & May Rudin Foundation, Inc.
The Rockefeller Foundation
Shubert Foundation
Starrett City Managed by Grenadier Realty Corp.
The Wallace Funds
Robert W. Wilson
The Norman & Rosita Winston Foundation

**PACESETTERS**
American Express Company
Rose M. Badgeley Residuary Charitable Trust
Mr. & Mrs. Charles M. Diker
The Henri & Eugenia Doll Foundation for the Performing Arts
Estate of Lois W. Davis
First Boston Corporation
Horace W. Goldsmith Foundation
William Randolph Hearst Foundation
Mrs. Alex Hillman
Family of Arthur Levitt, Jr. Philanthropic Fund
Marsh & McLennan Companies, Inc
Meet the Composer, Inc.
The Kathryn & Gilbert Miller Fund
Mr. Jan Mitchell
Mobil Foundation, Inc.
New York Magazine
Newsweek Inc.
Pfizer Inc.
Premiere Wine Merchants
Remy Martin Amerique
The Helena Rubinstein Foundation
The Scherman Foundation
Schlumberger
Emma A. Sheafer Charitable Trust
Steuben Glass
Michael C. Tuch Foundation
Uris Brothers Foundation

**PATRONS**
Best Products Foundation
Chappell Intersong Music Group
Mr. & Mrs. Neil D. Chrisman
CIGNA Corporation
Mr. & Mrs. Stephen J. Conway
Dillon, Read & Co., Inc.
Dime Savings Bank of New York
Donaldson Lufkin & Jenrette
Max & Victoria Dreyfus Foundation
Armand G. Erpf Fund
Mr. & Mrs. Mallory Factor
Mr. David Geffen
Mrs. Ira Gershwin
William & Mary Greve Foundation
Harkness Ballet Foundation, Inc.
The Heckscher Foundation for Children
Home Box Office, Inc.
IBM Corporation
Independence Savings Bank
Mr. & Mrs. Stanley H. Kaplan
Calvin Klein Ltd.
Mr. & Mrs. I. Stanley Kriegel
Mr. Mortimer Levitt
Mr. Edmund Littlefield Jr.
Mr. Hamish Maxwell
Ed & Sheila McDougal
McGraw-Hill Foundation
Merrill Lynch
Metropolitan Life Foundation
Henry & Lucy Moses Fund
Samuel I. Newhouse Foundation
Pepsico, Inc.
Ms. Alice Holbrook Platt
Nile Rodgers Productions
Rudin Management
Mr. Henry Schneider
Skidmore, Owings & Merrill
Tiffany & Company
Time Inc.
Amber Lightfoot Walker
Young & Rubicam Inc.

**CONTRIBUTORS**
Argenti, Inc.
Mr. Michael C. Bailkin
Educational Broadcasting Corp.
Estate of Anne Brier

General Electric Company
Global Sysco
Grace Foundation Inc.
Great Performances Party Coordinators
Ms. Agnes Gund
Florence & Herbert Irving
Irving One Wall Street Foundation
Ms. Jennifer U. Johnson
Johnson & Higgins
Mr. & Mrs. Lawrence B. Levine
Beulah & Martin Levine Foundation
Lord, Geller, Federico, Einstein
The Henry Luce Foundation
McKinsey & Co., Inc.
Mr. & Mrs. Richard L. Menschel
Morgan Stanley & Co., Inc.
Muidallap Corporation
Mr. & Mrs. Everett H. Ortner
The Parrish Art Museum
Quaker Sugar Co., Inc.
The Rockefeller Group
Salomon Inc
Ms. Pippa Scott
Evelyn Sharp Foundation
Silverstein Properties, Inc.
WNET

**THE NEXT WAVE PRODUCERS COUNCIL**

**Co-Chairmen**
Stephanie French
Amory Houghton III
**Vice Chairmen**
Alex Katz
Bette Midler
Gene Pressman
Roger Wallace
**Members**
Diane & Martin Ackerman
Mr. Allan Albert
Anonymous
Ms. Leslie Appleby
Dr. Sima Ariam
Mr. Michael C. Bailkin
Ms. Jennifer Bartlett
Mr. Om Batheja
Mr. Robert Beleson
Ms. Dianne Blell
Mr. Nelson Blitz, Jr.

21

# ANNUAL REPORT—Financial Summary

| Consolidated Balance Sheet Year Ended June 30, 1987 | FY1985# | FY1986# | FY1987# |
|---|---|---|---|
| **Assets** | | | |
| Current | | | |
| Cash | $ 379,616 | $ 65,656 | $ 89,649 |
| Cash in Reserve Account | 363,720 | 1,035,588 | 1,617,155 |
| Accounts Receivable | 67,047 | 247,580 | 568,016 |
| Grants Receivable | 731,709 | 879,236 | 1,638,880 |
| Prepaid Expenses | 691,978 | 516,557 | 1,288,468 |
| Total Current | $2,234,070 | $2,744,617 | $5,202,168 |
| Non-Current | | | |
| Grants Receivable | $ 157,500 | $ 226,429 | $ 285,000 |
| Fixed Assets (Net of Depreciation) | 1,308,027 | 1,378,827 | 1,425,397 |
| Total Assets: | $3,699,597 | $4,349,873 | $6,912,565 |
| **Liabilities** | | | |
| Current | | | |
| Notes Payable, Short Term | $ 100,000 | -0- | -0- |
| Capital Lease Obligation | 4,448 | -0- | -0- |
| Accounts Payable | 354,820 | 289,901 | 1,044,638 |
| Grants for Future Periods | 1,358,534 | 752,540 | 2,046,182 |
| Advance Box Office & Rentals | 244,049 | 353,605 | 266,203 |
| Total Current | $2,061,851 | $1,396,046 | $3,357,023 |
| Long Term | | | |
| Grants for Future Periods | $ 20,000 | $ 627,500 | $ 437,920 |
| Notes Payable | -0- | -0- | -0- |
| Capital Lease Obligation | -0- | -0- | -0- |
| Total Liabilities: | $2,081,851 | $2,023,546 | $3,794,943 |
| **Fund Balances** | | | |
| Unrestricted & Challenge Fund Balances Combined | $ 314,167 | $ 947,500 | $ 1,600,000 |
| BAM Majestic Theater Fund Balances | -0- | -0- | 92,225 |
| Fixed Assets | 1,303,579 | 1,378,827 | 1,425,397 |
| Total | $1,617,746 | $2,326,327 | 3,117,622 |
| Funds applied to deficit elimination and cash reserve | **$594,692** | **$708,581** | **$ 791,295** |

*#Summary of audited financial statements by the independent CPA firm, Lutz and Carr.*

24

| Consolidated Statement of Operations Year Ended June 30, 1987 | FY1985# | FY1986# | FY1987# |
|---|---|---|---|
| **Revenue** | | | |
| Box Office and Rentals and Concessions | $2,160,515 | $4,154,808 | $4,173,289 |
| Appropriations & Contributions | | | |
| New York City | 1,549,332 | 1,919,563 | 2,004,462 |
| New York State | 307,000 | 310,500 | 328,000 |
| Federal Support | 588,600 | 468,884 | 399,200 |
| Private Support | 1,967,250* | 2,524,565* | 2,898,999* |
| Capital Additions | 5,926 | 33,000 | 55,000 |
| NEA Challenge & Match | 718,546 | 694,140 | 518,931 |
| Total Revenue & Public Support | $7,297,169 | $10,105,460 | $10,377,881 |
| **Expenses** | | | |
| Program, Rentals, Concessions | $3,731,428 | $6,013,933 | $5,440,068 |
| Artistic Development | 467,941 | 640,115 | 315,873 |
| Program Related | | | |
| Stage & Production | 547,450 | 650,876 | 648,914 |
| Promotion, Advertising, Community Relations | 440,527 | 485,793 | 564,896 |
| House Management & Box Office | 167,213 | 184,196 | 324,453 |
| Building Maintenance & Operations | 534,141 | 576,316 | 1,156,965 |
| Administration | 242,634 | 268,769 | 329,344 |
| Development | 389,434 | 400,007 | 589,934 |
| Other Income/Expense (net) | 23,042 | -0- | -0- |
| Operating Expenses | $6,543,810 | $9,220,005 | $9,370,447 |
| Depreciation | 159,667 | 176,874 | 216,139 |
| Funds applied to deficit elimination and cash reserve | **$594,692** | **$708,581** | **$ 791,295** |

*#Summary of audited financial statements by the independent CPA firm, Lutz and Carr*
*\* This includes benefit income net of expenses*
*\*\* The excess of revenue over expenses reflects the National Endowment for the Arts Challenge Grant and matching funds which are restricted to deficit reduction and the establishment of a cash reserve fund*

25

# NEWSLETTERS

(Courtesy of The Brooklyn Academy of Music and of AFS Intercultural Programs, Inc.)

## INTRODUCTORY LETTER

Dear     :

Thank you very much for speaking with me on the telephone this afternoon about AFS' programs; I'm looking forward to meeting with you on Wednesday, 22 June at 11:00 a.m. In the interim, I am pleased to enclose a copy of our most recent Annual Report along with some additional information on our programs.

As you may know, AFS Intercultural Programs, the world's oldest and largest exchange organization, has been an active demonstrator of educational and cultural exchange as a means to transcend international boundaries and provide the groundwork for lasting peace. Since its founding in 1947 by World War I and II American Field Service volunteer ambulance drivers, over 160,000 young people and an equal number of host families have gained a profound understanding of other nations, other peoples, and themselves through their AFS participation.

With over 100,000 volunteers supporting activities internationally, the volunteer spirit of AFS' founders remains a crucial element in the operation of our programs. Programs throughout AFS' 70 country network are administered by paid professional staff and an extensive national volunteer structure. In the United States, over 2,500 local volunteer chapters help support AFS exchanges in 3,200 high schools. This past Program Year, approximately 10,000 participants and host families were involved in AFS exchanges throughout the world.

AFS programs encompass three broad themes: youth, education, and international development. Our youth programs—the largest area of activity—offer secondary school students the opportunity to live with a family and attend school in another country for a year or a summer. In the field of education, AFS has made great strides in its Visiting Teachers Program, in which high school teachers take an active role in the educational dialogue of over 17 countries including the People's Republic of China, Indonesia, Thailand, and various Latin American nations. And finally, in the area of international development, AFS operates special programs allowing for the free exchange of ideas and technology with nations and peoples in the developing regions of the world. Throughout all of these activities, AFS seeks to provide all participants with the strength, knowledge, and sensitivity necessary for the achievement of social justice and peace in a world of diversity.

As an international nonprofit organization, AFS is deeply affected by economic turbulence throughout the world and must seek support from nongovernmental sources such as individuals, foundations, and corporations. Many corporations in particular support AFS programs to provide their organizations with wide-reaching public exposure and to directly address the needs of their operating communities. Current corporate supporters such as (list several supporters here) have found that support of AFS not only generated excellent publicity for both external and internal groups, but also developed a source of future managerial talent. This has also helped to create a growing family of people motivated to contribute toward a more stable world in which to live and do business.

Current corporate involvement in AFS includes support of special programs such as the Urban Initiatives Program—a very successful project which provides the community outreach, financial aid, and counseling to enable economically disadvantaged students from inner city high schools to take part in AFS exchanges; Corporate Employee Scholarships which enable employee sons and daughters to take part in an AFS exchange; and support of our Teachers Exchange Program and Journalists Program. AFS media options to publicize corporate support have included company luncheons with company officials and AFS scholarship students, teachers, or journalists; listings in corporate newsletters and annual reports; and feature stories in AFS publications such as our alumni newsletter with a circulation of over 80,000 worldwide.

Given the ABC Corporation's many years of support of education and youth programs, I would very much like to get some of your suggestions and ideas on our current activities. I look forward to seeing you on the 22nd; please feel free to give my office a call in the interim if I can provide you with additional information.

Sincerely,

(Courtesy of AFS Intercultural Programs, Inc.)

# CORPORATE GENERAL-SUPPORT RENEWAL PROPOSAL

Dear

At a recent conference of the National Governors Association in Michigan, it was stressed that the United States needs to maintain an international perspective in all decisions, ranging from how we market our goods to how we educate our children. As all business markets become increasingly globalized—ideally leading to an era of new understanding and prosperity for all nations—no single country or region can afford to be in a position in which cultural conflicts and educational shortcomings can create serious obstacles to international communication and cooperation.

Since 1947, AFS Intercultural Programs has been expanding the horizons of countless individuals, families, and communities by building bridges for understanding in a world where international relationships are being strained to the breaking point. Many former AFS participants have achieved leadership positions in education, law, medicine, international business, and government, helping to solve problems, negotiate agreements, and resolve conflicts with a sensitivity and perspective of the world gained through AFS. Today, AFS continues to enable individuals throughout the world to realize the possibilities for cooperation in personal terms through their own experience with people from nations and cultures very different from their own.

Last year, your generous support in the amount of $ _____ enabled AFS to keep fees at a minimum, offer financial aid to deserving participants, and expand programs for young professionals. On behalf of the AFS Board of Trustees, I respectfully request that you renew your commitment this year to AFS by increasing your gift to $ _____ . Intercultural sensitivity and mutual understanding are not merely aesthetic principles, but are increasingly important ingredients in insuring positive global relations as well as profitable commercial ventures. Your renewed investment in AFS and the world's young people will help insure that the future will be more secure in their hands.

Sincerely,

(Courtesy of AFS Intercultural Programs, Inc.)

## CORPORATE SPECIAL PROJECT PROPOSAL

### THE AFS TEACHERS EXCHANGE PROGRAM

Proposal submitted to:
THE ABC CORPORATION
St. Paul, Minnesota

#### SUMMARY

AFS Intercultural Programs is a nongovernmental, nonprofit organization dedicated to increasing understanding of other cultures through worldwide exchange programs for students, professionals, workers, and families. Since its founding in 1947 by World War I and II American Field Service volunteer ambulance drivers, over 160,000 individuals and an equal number of host families in 70 countries have participated in AFS programs, transcending ideological, racial, and economic barriers through the person to person exchange of ideas and experience.

The focus of this proposal to the ABC Corporation is the expansion of the sending component of the AFS Teachers Exchange Program to specifically benefit teachers from the upper Midwest. This program involves an exchange of teachers from the United States living and working in Argentina, Chile, Costa Rica, Peru, the People's Republic of China, the Soviet Union, and Thailand—the teachers from these countries, along with Brazil, Colombia, Ecuador, the Dominican Republic, Guatemala, Honduras, Indonesia, Panama, Paraguay, and Venezuela, coming to the United States.

Since its beginnings in 1981, the teachers exchange has been primarily a U.S. hosting program, bringing foreign teachers to the United States. AFS is seeking to expand the sending of U.S. high school teachers abroad on the program to better meet the growing need in the United States for increased global education and to give U.S. teachers greater access to international professional experiences. Because the upper Midwest has been one of AFS' strongest regions in the U.S., the expansion of the U.S. sending component in this area could be easily accommodated through AFS' extensive network of chapters, volunteers, and educational contacts. Over the next three years, AFS projects that approximately 30% of the U.S. teachers sent abroad on the Program will come from this area.

AFS is seeking a challenge grant from the ABC Corporation in the amount of $ _____ to expand the sending of U.S. teachers from Minnesota and North Dakota, and to begin the sending of teachers from South Dakota. This funding will be matched one-to-one by contributions from individuals, corporations, and foundations nationwide.

#### THE NEED FOR GLOBAL AWARENESS IN THE UNITED STATES

At a time when contact between geographically distant and culturally divergent regions of the world is dramatically increasing through trade, investment, travel, and diplomatic ties, the majority of Americans are remarkably uninformed about other areas of the world. Many young Americans are particularly affected by the fact that U.S. secondary education often emphasizes Western European history, economics, and literature, giving only cursory attention to other regions such as Latin America and Asia. The foreign difficulties of recent years, from Vietnam to Iran, have demonstrated a need to greatly enhance American's knowledge of other languages and other cultures. This knowledge will also play a crucial economic role as the United States is further exposed to the competitive forces of international commerce. As all business markets become increasingly globalized—ideally leading to an era of new understanding and increased prosperity—the U.S. cannot afford to be in a position in which cultural conflicts and educational shortcomings can create serious obstacles to smooth international business relations.

(Courtesy of AFS Intercultural Programs, Inc.)

At a recent July conference of the National Governors Association in Michigan, it was stressed that the United States needs to maintain an international perspective in all decisions, ranging from how we market our goods to how we educate our children. The conference called for a reinstatement of foreign language proficiency as a college entry requirement; for a restoration of geography as a distinct subject in public schools; and for increased emphasis on competence in foreign studies among teachers. It has become a widely accepted fact that intercultural sensitivity and mutual understanding are not merely aesthetic principles, but are increasingly important ingredients in insuring positive global relations as well as profitable commercial ventures.

## THE NEED FOR SECONDARY LEVEL TEACHER REJUVENATION

Teachers clearly play key roles in increasing the international perspective of our future generations and very often provide the inspiration for students to reach their fullest potential. High school teachers especially can be pivotal individuals in the lives of our young people, and have an enormous influence on minds as they are just beginning to develop a mature awareness of the many possibilities for study and career. However, although a great deal of money, time, and energy has been spent in the United States for sabbatical and rejuvenatory programs for faculties at colleges and universities, up until now very little has been done for teachers at the secondary education level. Because of financial and scheduling restrictions, most high school teachers in the U.S. have little opportunity to travel and study abroad; without these "renewal" experiences, it becomes increasingly difficult for teachers to return to the classroom each September to teach and motivate their students.

## HOW AFS IS MEETING EDUCATIONAL NEEDS

The AFS Teachers Exchange Program has provided effective solutions to some of the challenges facing secondary education by giving U.S. teachers sorely needed opportunities to enhance their perspectives on subject matter and professional teaching sensibilities. These experiences make teachers better able to impart to their students the practical, emotional, and intellectual skills required to cope sensitively with the urgent challenges facing the next generation of adults.

Along with direct professional benefits for teachers, the AFS Teachers Program has been able to bring a sorely needed global viewpoint and awareness into classroom curricula in the United States and throughout the world. In recognizing this need, school boards, educational officials, and community leaders throughout the United States have embraced the AFS Teachers Exchange Program. The enthusiastic response of teachers, students, administrators, and school boards strongly indicates that the program provides a working model of ideas and concepts which can be used in the reshaping of teaching and learning in the U.S. and around the world.

## UNITED STATES TEACHERS ABROAD:

### Expansion in the Upper Midwest

Building upon the solid success of the United States hosting component for visiting foreign teachers, AFS is moving ahead to increase the number of U.S. teachers sent on the program, especially from well-established AFS regions in the United States such as the upper Midwest (Minnesota, North and South Dakota). Minnesota in particular has been for many years a very active AFS region with an extensive chapter structure and volunteer force; a network of 130 local AFS chapters and 167 high schools were key elements in the hosting and sending of 264 AFS students last year.

Many foreign visiting teachers have also been hosted in schools and communities in this area and have been linked with Master Teachers—key "host teachers" who help to integrate the visiting teacher into the school and coordinate the teacher's professional responsibilities. Because of their extensive experience as host coordinators and their exposure to international education, these Master Teachers are ideal candidates to be sent as U.S. teaching representatives to foreign classrooms.

During the current Program Year, 111 U.S. secondary school teachers will be hosted in Argentina, Chile, Costa Rica, the People's Republic of China, Peru, the Soviet Union, and Thailand. For the forthcoming two Program Years, it is projected that 163 and 200 U.S. teachers respectively will live and work abroad. Teachers from the United States depart for their foreign teaching assignments at the beginning of their summer vacations and are met personally by educational representatives in the host country. After orientation to their host country, the U.S. teachers travel to the schools and institutes to which they have been assigned.

*Goals.* The goals of the program for U.S. teachers are a) to enable the visiting U.S. teacher to achieve a greater understanding of the people, culture, and language of their host country; b) to provide the host school and community with a better understanding of the people, culture, and language of the United States; c) to interact with other teaching professionals and exchange ideas and techniques; and d) to serve as cultural resources in the U.S. teachers' areas of expertise.

*Recruitment.* Teachers in the United States are selected by AFS International and its volunteers throughout the U.S., assisted by Board of Education contacts at the state and local levels. Candidates for the program are teachers of foreign language, social studies, math, science, or physical education. AFS will give special preference to teachers that have served as Master Teachers to visiting AFS teachers from abroad.

*Orientation.* Several months in advance of the U.S. teachers arrival in their host country, they are sent a packet of information introducing them to their host culture as well as providing practical information on clothing, food, and accommodations. Two days prior to departure, departing teachers attend an orientation session at which lectures on culture, customs, crosscultural values, and educational systems are given (please refer to the section on expanded crosscultural orientation). Upon arrival in the host country, the U.S. teachers will have a four to seven day orientation and sightseeing program to further prepare them for their living and working experiences.

*Selection of Communities and Schools.* In Latin America and Thailand, U.S. teachers are placed with families and schools selected by the AFS National Offices, depending upon the needs of the hosting community. In the People's Republic of China, teachers are hosted at the leading foreign language institutes or universities in Beijing, Shanghai, Hunan, Jiangxu, and Tianjin, and live and take their meals in the foreign visitors quarters. In the Soviet Union, teachers are hosted at various educational institutes in Moscow and Leningrad.

*Professional Teaching Responsibilities.* Teachers are assigned one or several teaching activities depending upon the needs of individual schools and teacher's areas of expertise. U.S. participants in the program teach or assist in the teaching of English at different high school levels, and interact with students training to be English language teachers. In many foreign countries, especially in China and the Soviet Union, English language classes by and large stress reading, writing, and translation at the expense of conversing. The AFS visiting teachers from the United States will help fill this void by teaching conversational language courses, as well as giving an informed perspective on education, customs, and culture in the United States. Visiting teachers from the U.S. will also assist teachers of other subjects, depending on their language ability. Through the experience of teaching and interacting with colleagues in another culture, U.S. teachers will be able to obtain a better understanding of the process of imparting knowledge to a young audience, and will be better prepared to face many of the challenges of their own classrooms in the United States.

The intercultural experience gained by U.S. teachers working abroad has an especially strong impact on schools and students in rural areas of the United States. The predominance of rural areas in Minnesota, North Dakota, and South Dakota again make this region ideal for the sending of U.S. teachers on the Teachers Exchange Program. Very often, the contact young people from rural regions have with foreign culture is based upon stereotypes and less than accurate media reports. Teachers returning to their schools in these areas will be able to pass on to their students their direct educational experience in a foreign culture which is based not on preconception and fears, but on actual contact with another culture. The potential for opening up large populations of young people in all areas of the United States to this perspective, therefore, is one of the key goals of the program's sending component.

*Community Enrichment Activities.* Many opportunities for interaction in host communities are available to AFS participant teachers through AFS' extensive network of volunteers; enrichment activities will vary in each host country depending on local resources available. Living with host families (or with other teachers as is the case in China) will also give the U.S. teacher a great deal of direct access to the culture of the host country. Teachers are encouraged to participate at community cultural centers, to attend films, and to spend free time taking advantage of any other community activities which enable them to better know the particular host culture.

*Evaluation.* The Director of the AFS Center for Intercultural Learning will be overseeing the evaluation process and design of the questionnaire and interview format. Evaluations will take place in the U.S. upon teachers' return from their hosting assignments. In addition, AFS program staff will make periodic visits to the host communities to observe visiting teachers in action. Evaluation reports on these staff trips, together with the results of visiting teacher evaluations, will be used to make improvements on the program and make plans for future expansion.

## EXPANDED CROSSCULTURAL ORIENTATION TRAINING

The absolute foundation of any AFS program and the aspect that determines its success or failure more than any other is the quality of crosscultural orientation provided to participants. AFS, while having a great deal of experience in designing orientation sessions for young people from abroad, has recognized that orienting adult participants and their host families as well as professional educators at the host schools is a more complicated and very different proposition, one that requires a specially designed orientation reflecting the level of sophistication of all the participants.

At the core of all AFS experiences is the removal of people from their familiar environment and their placement in a new environment. In strange surroundings, the AFS participant is confronted repeatedly with crises of varying dimensions. He or she must make judgments and embark on actions in the absence of familiar cues. The visiting teacher will become fully involved in daily living and working arrangements with colleagues at the host school and with his or her host family.

Hosts too will be confronted with differences in basic living habits as well as subtle and complex differences in values, social norms, and patterns of thought. This is especially difficult in the fact of cultural stereotyping which has given us inconsistent and misleading information about many foreign cultures. The degree to which AFS can help all the participants turn these many and varied crises into opportunities for reassessing their own values, stretching their capacities, and learning and practicing new skills, the greater the success of the program.

U.S. teachers going on the Program begin their exchange experience with orientation training before they leave the United States at an international departure point (Miami for Central and South America, San Francisco or Los Angeles for Asia Pacific, and New York for the Soviet Union) conducted by AFS professional staff as well as experts in the areas of education, intercultural studies, and host country related issues. The pre-departure orientation sessions have been designed to accomplish three major objectives: a) to increase the teachers' competence in performing daily living activities as practiced in their prospective host countries ("survival skills"); b) to increase the participants' familiarity with their host society and educational system; and c) to increase their understanding of differing values and world views among cultures.

Selected topics to be covered at the orientations include:

- Introduction to themes in host cultures
- Transitions from U.S. to other cultures
- Teaching Methodologies: What methods can and cannot be transferred from U.S. classrooms to host classrooms
- Introduction to Educational Administration in the host country
- Daily habits of living in the host country: mail, telephone, money, meals, and hygiene
- Introduction to Life and Work in host secondary schools
- Ten tips for more effective teaching

The orientation activities will combine small group discussions, lectures using audio-visuals, roleplaying, and situation exercises. The orientations will be led ____ __ and will draw on the experience of other individuals in the field on intercultural education.

## THE FUNDING REQUEST

The total expenses for the United States sending component of the AFS Teachers Exchange Program for the three year period of September 1987 - August 1990 are $ _____ (approximately $ _____ per U.S. teacher). Of this amount, participation fees will cover $ _____ . We are turning to the ABC Corporation as well as individuals, foundations, and multinational corporations to support the AFS Teachers Program by helping to defray the $ _____ program cost to AFS. Although teacher participation fees help to defray the costs of program operation, AFS still assumes a major portion of expenses. The ABC Corporation's support for core costs will enable AFS to keep participation fees at a minimum, and will also provide funding for AFS to further reduce fees for teachers, expand pre-departure orientation programs in the U.S., and offer fellowship support in Minnesota, and North and South Dakota.

The Board of Trustees of AFS Intercultural Programs respectfully ask the ABC Corporation to join their efforts by making a three year challenge grant of $ _ _____ to help cover the costs of program expansion in Minnesota, North Dakota, and South Dakota. AFS' request to the ABC Corporation will be matched by individuals, corporations, and foundations, both in the upper Midwest and in other areas of the United States. Funding from the ABC Corporation would have a tremendous impact on the Program's growth both during and after its tenure by 1) firmly establishing the Program in Minnesota, North Dakota, and South Dakota; 2) enabling more teachers to have the financial ability to take part in the Program; 3) involving new funders from the corporate and foundation community in the United States to support the expanding U.S. sending program; and 4) to give AFS the time over the next three years to fully institutionalize fellowship costs into the internal and external budgeting priorities for the Teachers Exchange Program.

The ABC Corporation's grant of $ _____ could be earmarked by AFS in the following way: $ _____ in Year I, $ _____ in Year II; and $ _____ in Year III. When ABC Corporation funding terminates, AFS anticipates that substantial funding for program costs will be well established from new philanthropic support in the U.S. and increased budgeting through AFS. Your support during the next three years will enable AFS to expand its teachers program in the upper Midwest and other parts of the United States, *and* simultaneously keep participation fees for all teachers at a minimum, thus making the program accessible to more teachers whose salaries often prohibit them from taking part in travel and exchange programs.

Because of the central role that all teachers play as communicators in every society, AFS' exchange of educators is able to have a far-reaching impact in bringing about intercultural understanding and global awareness to large audiences. The increased accessibility and availability of the AFS Teachers Exchange Program will not only have a profound effect on the teachers directly involved, but literally on hundreds of students, families, and community members in the United States as teachers pass on what they have learned. By investing in this program, the ABC Corporation will play a vital role in supporting this expanded dialogue, and will help establish the building blocks for lasting world peace.

Included in the attachments is a budget for the program expenses involved in U.S. sending during the following three Program Years; information on teacher hosting and sending in Minnesota, North and South Dakota; and articles from local and national media sources

**PROPOSAL ATTACHMENTS**

1) Minnesota and North Dakota hosting schools
2) Minnesota U.S. teacher participants
3) Program budgets
4) U.S. teachers abroad—sending matrix
5) Local and national newspaper articles
6) Teachers Program supporters and prospects
7) AFS organizational operating budget
8) IRS 501 (c)(3) tax information
9) AFS International Board of Trustees
10) AFS Annual Report

## FOUNDATION SPECIAL PROJECT PROPOSAL

### THE NEXT WAVE PRODUCTION AND TOURING FUND

A Proposal to:
THE ABC MEMORIAL TRUST
NEXT WAVE PRODUCTION AND TOURING FUND

"It's a national shame that both Glass and Wilson must go to Europe to find a sympathetic set of producers for their world premieres."       Kay Larsen
New York Magazine
August 17, 1981

I. **Project Description and Request for Support**

The NEXT WAVE Production and Touring Fund's primary purpose will be to support the creation of major new works in this country from some of America's most important experimental artists, and at the same time encourage collaborations among them of potential significance. The Fund will support the production of these commissioned works as part of the Brooklyn Academy of Music's NEXT WAVE Festival and will provide funds that will enable the productions to tour extensively in the U.S., building a national audience for the artists and their work. The Fund will also support the development of a humanities/education program in conjunction with the BAM performances that will be made available to local sponsors for touring productions. Presenting the works in the context of the NEXT WAVE Festival at BAM will focus attention on the variety and the extraordinary creative activity in the experimental performing arts, attracting national and international media attention and generating important visibility for the artists' most significant large-scale works.

For the 1983-1984 season, the Brooklyn Academy of Music is projecting a need of $ _____ for the commissioning and production activities of the NEXT WAVE, $ _____ for the humanities/education project, $ _____ for administration, and $ _____ (net of income) to support the touring of productions, for a total of $ _____ . Most productions supported by the Fund will tour, some under BAM's auspices and some under the company's auspices—such as a Lucinda Childs tour booked by her management. The latter, referred to as affiliated touring, will credit the Fund's participation in the creation of the work. It is projected that tour support need will increase to $ _____ (net of income) in 1984-1985, since there will be more lead time to book tours. In 1985-1986, we are projecting a tour subsidy of $ _____ (net of income), with more extensive touring based on the groundwork established in previous years. In all of this work—commissioning, production planning, and touring—lead time is crucial in getting the works created, produced, and booked for tour. We are projecting a $ _____ fund by 1984-1985 and a $ _____ fund by 1985-1986 to cover growth that will take place in some aspects of the project each year. For this project, BAM respectfully requests support from the ABC Memorial Trust. It is our belief that the establishment of a fund at BAM to commission, produce, and tour works of America's most significant contemporary performing artists will be an event of some importance to American culture.

(Courtesy of The Brooklyn Academy of Music)

## II. Purpose

During the late 1960's and 1970's, an entire new generation of creative and experimental American performing artists began to make its presence felt in an exceptional and significant way. Composers such as Philip Glass and Steve Reich, choreographers including Laura Dean and Lucinda Childs, and theatrical artists such as director/designer Robert Wilson all reached a creative maturity and began to develop works of a large-scale, often collaborate nature that were heirs to a classical tradition, yet were radically new artistic statements. The major works of these new American artists, however, were rarely seen in the United States, and even more rarely performed outside of New York City. The works were not taken up by established American production companies and presentors due to their high costs and the inherent conservatism of these organizations. The fact that the works were created at all was due mainly to the commissions of forward-looking European artistic institutions. It would be an incalculable loss to the cultural life of this country if the efforts of these preeminent American artists continued to be unavailable to audiences across the U.S. at a time when widespread interest in their works has reached demonstrably major proportions.

The objective of the NEXT WAVE Production and Touring Fund is to develop and tour large-scale works by this new generation of creative artists, and to implement a corresponding humanities/education program as an integral part of this effort. It is our responsibility to provide these artists the opportunity to develop major works in the United States and to give these works visibility across the country. It is BAM's conviction that the establishment of this Fund would be a watershed for the contemporary performing arts in the United States.

## III. History and Rationale

There is a significant historical precedent in this century for the kind of special, large-scale collaborate works that the NEXT WAVE Festival seeks to commission and produce. In the early part of the twentieth century, Serge Diaghilev's Ballets Russes pioneered this kind of activity, bringing together such figures as Jean Cocteau, Erik Satie, Pablo Picasso, Leonide Massine, George Braue, Igor Stravinsky, Andre Derain, George Balanchine, Manuel deFalle, Georges Renault, Giorgia de Chirico, Michael Fokine, Darium, Milhaud, and Henri Matisse to contribute to his extraordinarily influential productions. Throughout her career, Martha Graham has worked with artists such as Aaron Copland, Norman Lloyd, Isamu Noguchi, Henry Cowell, Gian Carlo Menotti, Samuel Barber, and Wallingsford Riegger, producing commissioned works that have become universally acknowledged classics. Merce Cunningham, himself a member of Martha Graham's company in the 1940's, is the modern progenitor of the king of artistic collaboration that is proving to be such a vital creative form today. Cunningham's long-term artistic alliance with John Cage has profoundly affected contemporary thinking about the relationship of music and dance; and his work with such major American visual artists as Robert Raushenberg, Jasper Johns, Andy Warhol, Frank Stella, and Robert Morris, and composers Christian Wolff, Morton Feldman, LaMonte Young, and Conlon Nancarrow, to name just a few, is legendary. In 1969 the Brooklyn Academy of Music exhibited the first evidence of what has become a long-standing and unique commitment to the presentation of significant experimental work in this country when it produced Merce Cunningham's first major New York season. At that same approximate time, the work of many of the artists now associated with BAM's NEXT WAVE series first began to take shape. BAM presented four of Robert Wilson's epics in the early 1970's: *The Life and Times of Sigmund Freud, Deafman Glance, The Life and Times of Joseph Stalin,* and *The $ Value of Man.* BAM brought Julian Beck and Judith Malina's Living Theatre Lab and Peter Brook's Center for Theatre Research to this country, and brought Victor Garcia's production of *Yerma* from Spain. Twyla Tharp's involvement with BAM dates to the late 1960's, and Laura Dean has regularly been given the opportunity to develop her work at BAM since her performance of *Drumming* with Steve Reich in the mid-70's. More recently, BAM has presented sold-out performances of Philip Glass' opera *Satyagraha*; four performances of Lucinda Childs' Dance, with music by glass and setting by Sol LeWitt; choreographed work by Childs, Laura Dean, and Trisha Brown; the U.S. premiere of Laurie Anderson's complete *United States, Parts I-IV*; new work by Steve Reich; and commissioned Glenn Branca's *Symphony No. 3.*

Despite BAM's efforts in this area, many of the most important large-scale productions of these artists were commissioned and produced in Europe and have never, or rarely, been seen in the United States. The list includes Philip Glass in Robert Wilson's seminal *Einstein on the Beach*, which, financed by the artists themselves, toured extensively in Europe but played only two performances in this country at the Metropolitan Opera House in 1976; Robert Wilson's *Death, Destruction, and Detroit* and his *Golden Windows*, both of which were commissioned and produced in West Germany and neither of which has been seen in this country; Wilson's *Medea*, which has been co-commissioned by the opera companies of Lyon, Paris, and Venice; Glass' *Akhenaton*, a new opera commissioned by the Stuttgart Opera for production in 1984; Steve Reich's next major orchestral work, commissioned by the Cologne Orchestra (with BAM's NEXT WAVE as co-commissioner); Robert Ashley's *Perfect Lives*, a video opera that will be completed as a result of funding from England's new Channel 4; and even Glass' *Satyagraha*, which was commissioned by the city of Rotterdam and was seen (in the Netherlands Opera Production) in the U.S. for just five performances at BAM and three performances at Artpark.

The individuals responsible for these works are, by common consensus, among the most important creative artists of our time. In Europe these American artists are considered contemporary masters, and the productions of their works receive financial support far exceeding that which is received in the U.S. The institutional sponsors of the arts in this country must accept the responsibility to support our own most creative artists and to help make their work available to audiences across the country. It is also time that younger experimental artists—individuals such as Glenn Branca, Nina Wiener, Molissa Fenley, George Coates, and others—be given the opportunity to develop their work with the possibility of stimulating collaborations and growth. In conceiving this project, BAM is responding to substantial evidence that a significant audience has developed across the country for the work of these artists. *Einstein on the Beach* and *Satyagraha* sold out virtually every performance given in this country—a remarkable accomplishment for contemporary opera.

The nature of the audiences has also been unusual. Although his major theatrical works have had limited exposure in this country, Philip Glass and his ensemble have performed extensively, not only in concert halls but also in such unconventional locations as rock clubs and art galleries. The touring composer performing his or her own work is rare in this century, and this exposure to a wide-ranging audience has earned Glass a large, relatively young, non-academic following. This has similarly been the case with Steve Reich and Laurie Anderson. As a result, these artists have developed a popular and enthusiastic base of support for their work, the first such convergence of serious and popular acclaim on a national scale in decades.

Audiences across the country, however, have not had the opportunity to see these artists' most significant large-scale works; they have developed an interest in the artists only through exposure to smaller ensemble work or the abbreviated productions of touring dance companies. The touring of major stage works has not occurred because of the high costs of such ventures, and because of the skepticism of many sponsors regarding the experimental nature of the work. Nevertheless, the work of many of these artists is reaching a new creative peak, and it is our conviction that the time is right for an aggressive American approach to developing and touring this work. It is time for an American institution to take the lead in commissioning this work, arranging for its production, and encouraging its exposure in tours across the country. The work is important and mature enough to warrant this commitment, audiences have proven their desire to see it in many places across the country, and sponsors have begun to indicate a willingness to exhibit it, given some financial support.

As a result of its fifteen-year commitment to the experimental performing arts, BAM has developed a reputation as the most significant presenter of this kind of large-scale work in New York and across the country. Thanks in part to BAM's ongoing and long-standing commitment, the visibility and influence of a generation of American creative artists have reached new levels. It has already been indicated by many presentors across the country that BAM's imprimatur on a touring production would be an important asset in establishing the credibility of the production. We therefore feel that BAM is the logical initiator of this activity which will be of such great importance to the performing arts in America.

## IV.  NEXT WAVE Festival

After producing two seasons of work under the general framework of the NEXT WAVE, and sensing the timeliness of the project as outlined above, the Brooklyn Academy of Music plans to produce an annual NEXT WAVE Festival in the fall and early winter of the year which will involve the commissioning of new works, the production and presentation of those and other works, the development of a humanities program, the presentation of relevant films and exhibitions, and the occasional production of historical reconstructions that would provide a context for the Festival's progressive artistic activity. BAM's overall objective is to exhibit a wide-ranging array of artists involved in the experimental performing arts—including dance, music, music-theater, drama, performance art and other varied combinations of these disciplines—under the umbrella of the NEXT WAVE Festival. The Festival will utilize BAM's three performance spaces with both large-scale and smaller works by newer, younger artists as appropriate to each theater's configuration.

The majority of the works to be presented in the NEXT WAVE Festival will be discussed in detail in Section V.B. In addition to those works, other productions, which BAM will present but not produce, will also be a part of the NEXT WAVE Festival. However, because these works do not include a BAM producing and touring component, the Academy is not requesting support for these productions as part of the NEXT WAVE Production and Touring Fund.

**Advisory Council**

An Advisory Council has been set up for the NEXT WAVE Festival. This group of recognized leaders in the performing arts and related fields will work with BAM to recommend artists, suggest collaborations, and generally be available for advice in planning the Festival. The following are members of the Advisory Council.

Name—Title
Name—Title
Name—Title
Name—Title
Name—Title
Name—Title
Name—Title
Name—Title

This group, together with a larger, more informal network that BAM maintains, will keep the lines of communication open to important new works and artists.

## V. The NEXT WAVE Production and Touring Fund—Three-Year Plan

The NEXT WAVE Production and Touring Fund will help to underwrite the works described in Section V.B. Some of these works will be specially commissioned for the NEXT WAVE Festival, some will not; but the majority of them will tour subsequent to their performances at BAM. Before describing the specifics of the productions it is first necessary to clarify the touring aspects.

### A. Touring

As mentioned earlier, large-scale performance works by leading members of the American avant-garde are rarely viewed by audiences outside of New York City. Conversely, works by such artists as Philip Glass, Robert Wilson, Lucinda Childs, Lee Breuer, Steve Reich, Meredith Monk, and Laurie Anderson are given major presentations in municipal theaters and opera houses throughout Europe.

More people in Holland have seen Philip Glass' and Sol LeWitt's collaboration with Lucinda Childs, *Dance*, than in the United States.

Why? In essence, the Dutch government determined that in order to foster a healthy atmosphere for the creation of new work in the Netherlands, it was necessary to import the best artists and works from around the world. The best during the past decade have been American. For years, the virtues of American performance innovation have been marketed throughout Europe. Now it is time to bring home the artist-geniuses of this era.

The national performing arts marketplace is becoming increasingly sophisticated. Hundreds of theaters and centers offer annual series. Yet these series are predictably conservative. Unlike festivals or performing arts centers in Europe, American arts organizations are run from the box office up, rather than by artistic direction from the top. Programming is safe and, if promoted properly, cost-effective.

Genius is not necessarily cost-effective. It seems peculiar that a country founded on principles of frontierism and inspiration has not encouraged those concepts in the performing arts.

The Brooklyn Academy of Music is the only institution in America which has consistently presented large-scale performance works of great artistic achievement by new American artists. While the Walker Art Center in Minneapolis has presented an extensive program of avant-garde dance, music, and theater, these have been in the nature of extended residencies and small-scale performances.

Small-scale works have toured in the USA for the past several years. Companies such as the Philip Glass Ensemble (music), Mabou Mines (theater), and Laura Dean Dancers and Musicians (dance) have managed two to six weeks of touring annually in America. However, these companies do not take their most dynamic or largest-scale works on the road. Top fees available to Mabou Mines, for example, have not exceeded $ _____ per performance, even at the most well-endowed venues. The income from an average of four to give performances a week, under the best circumstances, dictates the size of the production which can be toured. The company would have to include no more that seven members in order for such a tour to be cost-effective. When the Philip Glass Ensemble toured America in March of 1982, it presented a music repertory in seventeen cities from Baltimore to Los Angeles. The average theater had 1,250 seats. The Ensemble sold out eight of these halls, while averaging 70% capacity throughout the tour. Glass traveled with five musicians, three technicians, a road manager, and an equipment truck. The per-venue fee averaged $ _____ . The entire tour barely broke even. Ten of the cities on the tour had never before hosted the Philip Glass Ensemble.

*The Photographer/Far from the Truth*, with music by Philip Glass, direction by JoAnne Akalaitis of Mabou Mines, and choreography by David Gordon, has a company of 31 performers and technicians, and a per-performance fee of $ _____ . The presenters who have had difficulty with a $ _____ fee for the Ensemble are the same ones who are prime candidates for *The Photographer/Far from the Truth* and/or Lucinda Childs' repertory.

As the 1982 Philip Glass tour proved, audiences will turn out for the American avant-garde if it is promoted and marketed well. The task at hand is to make the full-scale versions of his work and those of Wilson, Reich, Anderson, etc., available to this interested public.

There will be two kinds of touring productions sponsored by the Fund. The first will be those productions toured under BAM's auspices and booked by a firm with professional touring experience in both the business side of touring as well as the logistical and stage management areas. Moreover, BAM will contract with a firm whose past work has been involved with many of the NEXT WAVE artists so that their knowledge and interest should enhance their effectiveness in booking and in providing a package of marketing support materials for the local presenter.

The subsidy for touring productions would support tour dates where there is a legitimate gap between the presenter's ability to pay and the cost of the presentation. The firm hired to book the tour will receive a commission based on the fees paid so that they will have every incentive to stretch the subsidy as much as possible. Obviously, the presentors will differ in their ability to pay, and also there will be venues where special consideration would be appropriate for one reason or another.

The second type of touring will involve those works produced by BAM that will tour in an affiliated way. For example (unless it is agreed the *Set and Reset* will be toured under BAM's auspices), Trisha Brown's collaboration with Laurie Anderson and Robert Rauschenberg—currently a scheduled part of the 1983-1984 Festival—could eventually tour as one element of the Trisha Brown Dance Company's regular touring program. In such cases, the work in question will be clearly identified as having been made possible by the NEXT WAVE Production and Touring Fund.

In the case of subsidized touring, production expenses associated with developing each new work will be divided; fifty percent of the expense assigned to "production" and fifty percent assigned to "touring". This division represents a realistic allocation of the up-front costs needed to launch each work and make it available for touring.

B. **Commissions and Productions**

The following projects, which will be part of the NEXT WAVE Festival, come under the purview of the Fund:

1983-1984
1. *The Photographer/Far from the Truth*—This music-theater work is a free adaptation of an idea conceived by Rob Malasch and originally produced by the Holland Festival in 1982, with music by Philip Glass and a new script by Robert Coe. The piece is based on the life and work of Eadweard Muybridge, whose pioneering sequential studies of locomotion made him known as the "father of the motion picture." BAM is planning a production with JoAnne Akalaitis as director and David Gordon as choreographer. The work is one and one half to two hours in length and will be designed to tour. The music was composed last year and was issued on CBS Records several months ago. The scenario includes a dramatization of parts of Muybridge's life and a visualization of his work in part by dancers and in part by projections of his photographs. The music is rich and beautiful, and the anticipation of having Akalaitis and Gordon work together is a most exciting prospect.

Production Cost: $

Touring Cost: $                          Touring Income: $

2.  *Lucinda Childs*—Lucinda Childs and her dance company will present the New York premiere of *Available Light*, which is being co-commissioned by BAM and the Museum of Contemporary Art in Los Angeles as a mutual collaboration between Ms. Childs, composer John Adams, and architect Frank Gehry. Also included will be the New York premiere of *Mad Rush* with a score by Philip Glass and costumes by Carol Murashige.

    Production Cost: $

    Touring Cost: $            Touring Income: $
    (Affiliated)                 (Affiliated)

3.  *The Gospel at Colonus*—This production was conceived by Lee Breuer and Bob Telson and will be directed by Mr. Breuer. Music is by Mr. Telson with sets, costumes, and lighting by Alison Yerxa. Sophocles' classic drama, *Oedipus* at Colonus, has been transformed into a contemporary gospel/theater piece, blending the black church service, as one of the roots of American music, with the staged choral ode presenting the essence of Greek tragedy as a religious experience. The story of Oedipus' redemption at Colonus is set in a gospel service and features major gospel groups such as the Five Blind Boys of Alabama and J. J. Farley and the Original Soul Stirrers. The production, produced in association with the Walker Art Center and Liza Lorwin, will be developed in a workshop format in Minneapolis before its premiere at BAM.

    Production Cost: $

    Touring Cost: $            Touring Income: $

4.  *Trisha Brown/Laurie Anderson/Robert Rauschenberg*—The Trisha Brown Dance company will perform the world premiere of *Set and Reset*, a collaborate work by these three artists. *Set and Reset*, with Ms. Anderson performing her original score live and Mr. Rauschenberg's visual presentations and costumes, continues Ms. Brown's collaborative efforts with visual artists and composers. Discussions are under way to include *Set and Reset* in the 1984-1985 NEXT WAVE tour.

    Production Cost: $

    Touring Cost: $            Touring Income: $

5.  *Nina Wiener/Judy Pfaff*—Nina Wiener and Dancers will present the world premiere of Wind Devil, an evening-length work. Created in commemoration of the centennial anniversary of the Brooklyn Bridge, the piece will have decor designed by visual artist Judy Pfaff with original music commissioned especially for the work, by composer Sergio Cervetti, incorporating sounds taken from the Great Bridge. This premiere marks Ms. Wiener's first collaboration with a visual artist.

    Production Cost: $

    Touring Cost: $            Touring Income: $
    (Affiliated)                 (Affiliated)

6.  *Molissa Fenley/Anthony Davis*—Choreographer Molissa Fenley and her ensemble, Molissa Fenley and Dancers, in collaboration

with composer/pianist Anthony Davis and his ten-musician ensemble Episteme, will present the world premiere of *Hemispheres*. Costume will be designed by Rei Kawakubo, and the visual element will be created by Francesco Clemente.

Production Cost: $

Touring Cost: $                    Touring Income: $
(Affiliated)                       (Affiliated)

**7. Other engagements included in the Festival which will not be commissioned but will be presented, are *The Way of How*, a music-theater piece by Paul Dresher and George Coates; *Victory over the Sun*, a recreation of the celebrated 1913 Russian Cubo-Futurist opera; dancers/choreographers Rina Shenfeld and Carolyn Carlson; and the Art Ensemble of Chicago.

(**Funds for the NEXT WAVE Production and Touring Fund will not be applied to these projects since they are presentations only and have not been commissioned by BAM.)

*1984-1985* (Examples of potential large-scale projects)
1.  *Einstein on the Beach*—one of the most influential music/theater works of the 1970's, Robert Wilson and Philip Glass' opera played for only two performances in this country, both at the Metropolitan Opera House. Both Wilson and Glass are committed to re-creating the work for the 1984 Festival and for a subsequent tour.

    Production Cost: $

    Touring Cost: $                Touring Income: $

2.  *The Desert Music*—A 60-70 minute work by Steve Reich is being co-commissioned by the Cologne Orchestra and BAM. It is being scored for a large orchestra (about 90 players) and a chorus of 14, and has as its text poetry of William Carlos Williams. We are negotiating with Michael Tilsom Thomas to conduct the Brooklyn Philharmonic Orchestra for these performances.

    Production Cost: $

    Touring Cost: $                Touring Income: $

There will be other large and small projects which will be developed over the next year for the 1984 Fall Festival. The activity of the 1984 Festival will be at least as extensive as that planned for 1983. In addition, expanded touring of the three pieces mentioned above is being planned since there will be lead time for booking. Obviously, a touring schedule is impossible to draw up now for the 1984-1985 season, but the 1983-1984 touring program is an abbreviated model of what can be done in future years, with the further ability to expand.

*1985-1986* (Example of a potential large-scale project)
1.  *Title of New Opera*—A Name/Name commissioned opera. This will be the second major collaboration of these artists, (amount) years after they created *Name of Opera*.

The remaining projects for the fall of 1985 and for touring will be generated within the next eighteen months. The scope of the commissioned and produced work will be similar to that of the previous years and it is expected that the touring will expand.

### VI.  Humanities/Education Program

As an integral part of the NEXT WAVE Festival, the Brooklyn Academy of Music has organized and will be implementing a humanities/education program. The Academy's experience with a similar program, which served the 1980-1981 season of the BAM Theater Company, demonstrated the receptivity on the part of both academic and general-public audiences to materials and events that enrich and amplify the aesthetic experiences of the performances themselves.

Given the experimental nature of the NEXT WAVE presentations, one of the prime thrusts of such a humanities program will be to locate the position of the NEXT WAVE within the tradition of the avant-garde and artistic innovation in the twentieth-century. Through a consideration of such movements as Surrealism, Futurism, Dadaism, Constructivism, and the Bauhaus, and particularly the performing arts collaborations between major visual, musical, literary, and choreographic artists which were such an integral part of such phenomena, an important perspective on the works commissioned for the NEXT WAVE could be gained. for example, the collaborations between Satie, Massine, Cocteau, and Picasso on *Parade*; Prokofiev, Kochno, Balanchine, and Drouault on *Prodigal Son*; and Martha Graham with Isamu Noguchi and Samuel Barber and Aaron Copland, to name only a few, could place in context and illuminate a piece by Twyla Tharp and Philip Glass or a Trisha Brown/Laurie Anderson/Robert Rauschenberg collaboration.

Such concepts as minimalism, performance art, and the theater of images, which are often raised in regard to the NEXT WAVE artists could be explored both in historical and contemporary terms. In addition to examining these ideas in relation to the works of art themselves, parallels with divergent but related fields could be established. For example, an invitation to major practitioners of contemporary literary theory (and such concepts as semiotics and deconstruction) like Michel Foucault, Jacques Derrida, Harold Bloom, Geoffrey Hartman, and Paul De Man to attend and discuss the work of Wilson, Glass, Anderson, et. al., might prove to be a fascinating experiment in humanistic cross-fertilization.

Even more interdisciplinary type discussions are possible in regard to this provocative material. Since the terms dream, trance, and hypnotic state are often used to describe the music of Glass and Reich, the theater of Robert Wilson, and the choreography of Laura Dean and Lucinda Childs, the psychological dimensions of their aesthetic could be probed. In an interview Philip Glass is quoted as saying, "Couldn't we say that a lot of the trouble with avant-garde music in the sixties was that it was written for the wrong side of the brain?" suggesting that his music is directed toward the nonintellectual right side of the brain. Since much important work is being done on researching the differing properties of the two hemispheres of the brain, the physiological impact of such music is another area the humanities program could explore. Pioneers in the field of brain research such as Harvard neurologist Norman Geschwind and University of Chicago biopsychologist Jerry Levy could be called upon to discuss the provocative topic of music and the brain.

In more traditional terms, the NEXT WAVE commissions in music, opera, dance, and theater will serve as the basis of important considerations of the relationship between these works and the established corpus of twentieth-century work in these fields.

Since Philip Glass studied with Nadia Boulanger in Paris, for example, a symposium might explore the contribution of Ms. Boulanger on influencing modern music through such composers as Aaron Copland, Virgil Thompson, and Elliot Carter, as well as Philip Glass. This same discussion could them center on the ways in which Glass's music has moved away from their paths. A different but related discussion might compare the music of Glass, Steve Reich, and Terry Riley with earlier composers like Charles Ives, Henry Cowell, and John Cage, especially as their work differs from other modern composers like Luciano Berio, George Crumb, Pierre Boulez, and Karlheinz Stockhausern. And since Glass has also acknowledged a strong influence by nonwestern musical forms, a consideration of those influences on both his work and that of other contemporary artists could be planned.

With the theater pieces, the phenomena of performance art could be juxtaposed with Futurist *serate*, the work of Breton, Cocteau, and Artaud and happenings, while the theater of images and minimalism could be compared with the theatrical metaphors of Beckett, Ionesco, and Arrabal. Since Robert Wilson's work is strongly concerned with visual images, the contribution of theatrical design to twentieth-century theatrical expression could be assessed through a combination of exhibits, lectures, and symposia and articles and monographs. These programs would also, of course, be able to include the work of artists like Robert Rauschenberg who are participating in the NEXT WAVE collaborations.

In dance-related activities, the relationship between the NEXT WAVE choreographers—Laura Dean, Trisha Brown, Lucinda Childs—as well as such major figures as Martha Graham, Merce Cunningham, and Paul Taylor, could be studied as part of a major effort to determine the ways in which NEXT WAVE choreography has roots in dance history and how and where it has chosen to forge new directions.

**Project Components**

The humanities/education program will contain four major components.

1)  *LITERATURE*

     *Audience guide/magazine*: The experience with INSIDE, the audience magazine which BAM produced and distributed for the five productions of the 1980-1981 Theater Company season demonstrated that audiences for performing arts events which provide more than "escapist" entertainment are eager for materials that can provide background information and amplification for the performance itself. Thus, for NEXT WAVE events, BAM would publish a magazine/guide along the lines of the INSIDE publication.

     This magazine/guide would try to approach the individual pieces in a manner that is both illuminating and entertaining. Visual material would be utilized to the fullest extent possible, with the magazine/guide designed by a first-class graphic artist. The articles would be collected and commissioned from a wide variety of sources, both academic and nonacademic. Whenever possible, interviews with the creative artists involved in the collaborations would be featured, along with considerations of their past work.

     *The Photographer/Far from the Truth* can be used to cite examples of what a NEXT WAVE magazine/guide might contain. Interviews with Philip Glass, Robert Coe, JoAnne Akalaitis, and David Gordon could explore their approaches to the material, how the collaboration proceeded and how the piece evolved into rehearsal. A background article could explore Eadweard Muybridge's contribution to the history and development of photography, with accompanying examples of his work. In addition, essays on the previous work of Glass, Gordon, Akalaitis, and the Mabou Mines could be solicited from a musicologist and dance and theater historians to present the readers with an artistic context within which *The Photographer/Far from the Truth* could be viewed.

This guide/magazine would be sent in advance to subscribers to the NEXT WAVE Festival and made available to groups and single-ticket purchasers. The experience with the BAM Theater Company INSIDE magazine showed that audience members, teachers, and students found it useful when read either before or after attending the performance. Copies of the magazine would also be part of the tour package and would be distributed to the arts organizations presenting the productions throughout the country.

2)   *PUBLIC EVENTS*
*Post-performance discussions*: Audiences will be invited to remain after selected BAM and tour city performances of NEXT WAVE events to participate in discussions with the artists. These discussions may be in the form of panels moderated by an expert in the field and featuring the participation of other scholars and critics who would then interact with the artists and audience members. Other discussions might be more informal in nature, allowing the director of the humanities program to present the artists to the audience in order to answer questions and to discuss the audience's reaction to the piece. One subscription series might be designated as a discussion series, so that attendees at those performances would be able to participate in a discussion after each event. Whatever form the discussions took, they would provide an opportunity for a dialogue and exchange of ideas on the NEXT WAVE productions.

*Activities for younger audience*: Certain NEXT WAVE pieces would be offered to high school audiences to expose students to experimental work in the performing arts. Perhaps special matinee performances would be scheduled, followed by a discussion. In addition to the audience guide/magazine, special material of particular interest to high school teachers and students would be prepared and disseminated. These study guides would suggest in-school projects to be undertaken before attendance at the performance and follow-up activities. In certain cases either before or after classes attended the performance for lecture/demonstrations and more in-depth discussion.

*Symposia, seminars, lectures, etc.*: Special attempts will be made to involve members of local colleges and universities in NEXT WAVE activities. This participation will involve not only attendance at performances and at the subsequent discussions but also the planning of major intellectual programs that consider the larger esthetic and humanistic issues raised by NEXT WAVE events. The appearance of the small, experimental dance companies from Holland, Italy, and Israel could form the basis for a symposium on Contemporary Dance in Europe and the United States, perhaps sponsored in conjunction with Dance Theatre Workshop and the dance programs of either New York University's Tisch School of the Arts or the SUNY Purchase campus. A major symposium on the work of Robert Wilson, including pictorial displays, might be planned in conjunction with the CUNY Ph.D. program in theater. A seminar on Schoenberg-Webern-Berg and the relationship between serialism and atonality and the work of Philip Glass could be presented in conjunction with the music departments of the University of California at Berkeley and Stanford University if one of the Glass collaborations were to be presented at either (or both) of these Bay Area institutions.

3) *OUTREACH*
*Gallery Exhibitions and Historic Reconstruction*: Special exhibitions will be organized and mounted to present designs, manuscripts, dance notation and related visual material by and relating to Festival artists. These exhibitions would be on display in selected metropolitan New York museums and galleries and would also be sent out to tour locations. A Rauschenberg exhibition would be mounted to coincide with the appearance of his piece. An exhibit of Ballets Russes designs would point out the historic precedence for NEXT WAVE collaborations. A Muybridge exhibit, along with special showing of the film *Eadweard Muybridge*, could accompany the presentation of *The Photographer/Far from the Truth*. These exhibitions would also include the reconstruction of important historic materials relevant to avant-garde movements in the arts.

4) *ARCHIVES*
The Academy plans to make fixed-camera video documents of each event in the Festival. The video tapes will be stored at the Academy and will form the basis of an important library collection comprising the only complete record of the experimental works being presented in the NEXT WAVE. Higher quality recordings of the musical material could also be included in the archives, along with all publications and critical response generated by the Festival events. Tapes of interviews conducted for the guide/magazine and other materials would also enter the collection.

**PROJECT IMPLEMENTATION**

Dr. Roger Oliver has been appointed director of the humanities program to work closely with the Festival coordinator and the Academy staff. Dr. Oliver is responsible for the preparation of the audience guide/magazine and all other written materials, including any substantive portions of the in-house theater program. He will also organize the post-performance panels and discussions and act as liaison between the artists and the academic participants in the humanities program events in New York. He will also provide ideas and all possible assistance to the organizers of the tour city appearances.

In addition, Dr. Oliver will work closely with the NEXT WAVE Advisory Council in general and the humanities subcommittee in particular. Those members of the Council with particular academic and humanistic interest will form the subcommittee which will oversee the activities of the humanities program. Members of such a subcommittee include:

Name—Title
Name—Title
Name—Title
Name—Title

Dr. Oliver is a distinguished academic humanist with knowledge of the history of the performing arts and contemporary theater, opera, music, and dance.

## VII. Administration

The NEXT WAVE Festival administration consists of a coordinator and a humanities director. This office is responsible for scheduling, contracting, and producing the Festival as well as developing materials and activities. They will work closely with Harvey Lichtenstein and the Advisory Council on programming and commissioning, and on the development and realization of an integral humanities program; the BAM Production Office on all technical aspects of the productions and events; the BAM Marketing Department on press, promotion, and marketing; the BAM Planning Department on fundraising, project proposal preparation, and reporting; and the firm hired to book the tour, as the liaison for touring. The coordinator for the NEXT WAVE Festival is Mr. Joseph Melillo and he is directly responsible to Mr. Lichtenstein.

While the Festival will take place over a three-month period, the amount and variety of activity in BAM's three theaters, plus the development of a comprehensive educational component, warrant a full-time staff. As the Festival develops, it is expected that there will be a greater emphasis on commissioning and producing, since that is the area of greatest need for contemporary artists. Developing and producing a work is much more demanding than presenting it. Already, BAM is more heavily into commissioning and producing for the Festival than it has generally been in the past.

## VIII. Evaluation

An evaluation of the success of the activities sponsored by the NEXT WAVE Production and Touring Fund naturally involves a combination of objective and subjective judgments. The Fund's most important result—the creation and production of a series of major new works by some of this country's most significant experimental artists—can be measured in terms of the number of these works created, but it must also be measured by subjective criteria that the contribution of such a body of new works makes to our culture.

There are, however, a number of ways in which to evaluate the success of the project. Attendance and box office figures for NEXT WAVE events, both at BAM and on tour, would be compiled and compared on a year-to-year basis as the most obvious means of determining the Fund's impact. The number of tour performances and the geographical outreach of the program (i.e. the number of different communities reached) would also be compiled on an ongoing basis.

Another method both of interpreting success and, more importantly, providing tour sponsors with assistance in their own efforts, is the analysis of the BAM NEXT WAVE audience. BAM has recently installed a Hewlett Packard 3000 Series 30 computer system and has an information specialist on staff to supervise its use. Audience surveys designed and analyzed with the aid of the computer would not only generate useful demographic data, but also provide information that would be exceptionally useful in targeting both BAM's and local sponsors' marketing campaigns for NEXT WAVE events. Such surveys would also be prepared for selected touring events for an even greater degree of accuracy and more thorough selection of information. BAM would additionally measure the impact of the humanities segment of the project by surveying those who had participated in the humanities programs and those who had not.

The project's success would also be measured in terms of critical response and the general level of visibility, both nationally and internationally, that the Festival and the tours achieve for the artists and their work.

# AFFINITY CARD MAILING

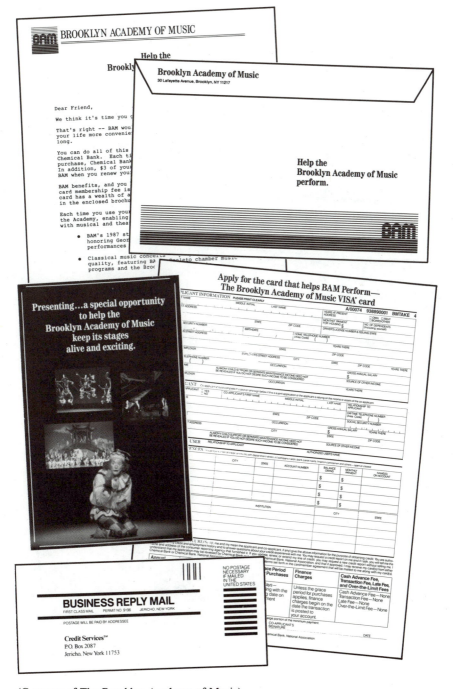

(Courtesy of The Brooklyn Academy of Music)

## SEAT ENDOWMENT BROCHURE

(Courtesy of The Brooklyn Academy of Music)

## DIRECT-MAIL PACKAGE I—Letter

Date

*"When we are young, we wear our ideals on our t-shirts–then, we grow older and wear them out. But it is only when we are older that our young ideals can bring real value to the world–for we are finally smart enough and strong enough to put them into action. But sadly, most people never savor the sweetness of their ideals because they stumble over how, when and where to do something-anything."*

—An AFS Alumnus—

Dear Friend,

Fortunately, the world has AFS. And AFS has you! That's why we are asking you to renew your commitment to the ideals which can help to change the world, a person at a time.

Every year thousands of AFSers share the education, language, work, and interests of other societies and demonstrate how open minds and a willingness to experience is the essence of intercultural understanding. They discover diversity as a source not of conflict, but of learning and strength. And that nothing is impossible.

Over half of the 9000 AFS participants in 1985 received some form of financial assistance. Young people from families and countries with lower economic capabilities were able to participate thanks to funds raised by volunteers in local chapters and national organizations all over the world. These sources world-wide only cover a portion of all program operation costs. So this year AFS must raise the funds to bridge the $1.15 million dollar "gap."

And this is why AFS is asking you, as an individual, to renew the gift you made last year and to consider increasing your contribution if at all possible. For we must continue to feed the hopes of the young with the strength of experience.

Please take a moment to renew your gift today. And let a friend know about AFS. Because that's how the world changes, a person at a time.

Warm regards,

(Courtesy of AFS Intercultural Programs, Inc.)

## DIRECT MAIL PACKAGE I—Brochure and Reply Card

## DIRECT-MAIL PACKAGE II

Brooklyn Academy of Music
30 Lafayette Avenue
Brooklyn, N.Y. 11217

Harvey Lichtenstein
President and
Chief Executive Officer

Dear Neighbor:

You are standing in the middle of an empty stage. The theater is dark and quiet. One bare light bulb illuminates the empty wings and back wall.

Suddenly you hear the magnificent voices of Enrico Caruso and Geraldine Farrar in Gounod's Faust. Looking into the darkness you see the movements of Isadora Duncan, Pavlova and Nijinsky. You watch as a young dancer named Rudolf Nureyev astounds the audience in his New York debut.

Look and listen for the recent masterful performances by Paul Taylor, Jason Robards, Alvin Ailey, Twyla Tharp, Philip Glass and many more. Here, on this stage, these great talents were presented to New York, America, and the World.

You are standing on an empty stage in a dark theater, a stage that has presented the finest in theater, music, film and dance for one hundred and twenty-one years. You are in fact standing on the stage of the oldest performing arts center in America, the Brooklyn Academy of Music, a stage that should never be empty.

The lights will be lit and the stage will be set this season for over 230 performances, thanks to the Friends of BAM, individuals such as yourself who are concerned with keeping BAM full of the very best in performing arts. This season the Friends of BAM are filling BAM's four stages with an incredible array of exciting performances and premieres.

BAM's Ballet International will fill the Opera House with New York and American premieres performed by The Norwegian National Ballet, The Cullberg Ballet Company of Stockholm, the Dutch National Ballet, The Basel Ballet, the Hamburg Ballet, and the London Contemporary Dance Theater.

The Next Wave: New Masters at The Brooklyn of Music, a continuation of the contemporary music and dance series that won national attention last fall will include performances by Laurie Anderson, Robert Wilson, Steve Reich and Jessye Norman, among others.

(Courtesy of The Brooklyn Academy of Music)

## TELEFUNDRAISING RENEWAL SCRIPT

Good Evening, Mr./Mrs. _____ . This is _____ calling from the Brooklyn Academy of Music. (How are you this evening?)

We're calling, Mr./Mrs. _____ , for two reasons. First, we'd like to thank you for your past support. You may not realize it, but our ticket prices cover only half of our production costs. The other half is covered by grants and gifts from generous people like yourself. Thank you very much for your help.

The second reason for the call is to personally invite you to renew your membership as a FRIEND OF BAM. To show our appreciation for a gift of (*One Level Above Previous Gift*) you'll receive many of the benefits you're familiar with like invitations to working rehearsals, plus a few additional ones as well! (Explanation of relevant premiums.)

Can I renew your membership at the $ _____ Level?

[Go to closing or objections]

(Courtesy of The Brooklyn Academy of Music)

## TELEFUNDRAISING ACQUISITION SCRIPT

Hello, may I speak to (USE FULL NAME), please?

Good evening, Mr./Ms. _____ . This is (YOUR FULL NAME) calling from the Brooklyn Academy of Music. (How are you this evening?)

*FOR INSIDE LISTS*
Mr./Ms. _____ , I understand you have attended (BAM, our Next Wave Festival, etc.) in the past.
- is that correct?
- and what did you see here?
- what did you think of it?
- did you enjoy it?

(Well,) Mr./Ms. _____ , as you may be aware, last year BAM celebrated our 125th anniversary as America's oldest performing arts institution. This year, with the help of our friends, we've inaugurated the BAM Majestic, a newly refurbished theatre which brings our performance spaces to a total of four.

We're calling this evening, Mr./Ms. _____ , to invite you to join the Friends of BAM, a support group that helps us to defray the high costs of bringing you innovative programming, while allowing us to maintain our low price ticket policy. It also allows us to continue our important education programs.

Mr./Ms. _____ , you can become a member of the Friends of BAM with only a $75.00 contribution. To show our appreciation for your support, you will receive a whole series of benefits and privileges, such as two invitations to each scheduled working rehearsal over the next 12 months. These rehearsals offer a fascinating look at the creative process and are open by invitation to our Friends only.

You also receive an invitation for you and your guest to a special Friends of BAM Donor Reception which I hear may be attended by some of our major artists. Plus, we will send you a complimentary print of the striking 1987 Next Wave Festival Poster by Willem de Kooning, a copy of the Next Wave Festival Journal, a membership card entitling you to a 20% discount at the BAMSHOP, and access to an exclusive telephone line for ticket and scheduling information.

(Courtesy of The Brooklyn Academy of Music)

So, will you join us with a $75.00 contribution, Mr./Ms. _____ ?

NO

Why would you hesitate? (GO TO APPROPRIATE RESPONSE, OR SECOND CLOSE)

## SECOND CLOSE

Mr./Ms. _____ , have you ever heard of our education programs? (PAUSE) Well, I'm not surprised; I don't think we tell enough people about the 120,000 school children we reach *every* year with BAM's daytime Performing Arts Program for Young People. So many thousands of our city's children depend on BAM for their first exposure to the magic of the live performing arts.

The point is, without support from many people like you, we might be in danger of losing one of New York's finest offerings in the performing arts *and* arts education.

Now, I have your address here as (CONFIRM ADDRESS, SPELLING OF NAME, ETC.). Is this correct?

(PAUSE...THEY MUST SAY THE NEXT WORD)

Good! NOW, we can confirm your gift with any of the major credit cards: American Express, Visa, and Mastercard. Which card will this be on?

(PAUSE...THEY MUST SAY THE NEXT WORD)

FOR "SALE", GO TO SALE

## SALE

(CONFIRM ADDRESS)

CREDIT CARD: And what is the card number?
And the expiration date?
Let me read that back to you. (READ BACK)

CHECK GIFT: (AFTER ATTEMPTING TO OVERCOME OBJECTIONS) That's fine, Mr./Ms. _____ . I wonder, however, if you can do me a favor. Do you have your checkbook nearby? (PAUSE) It would be very helpful to us if you can write in the "notes" section on the check: TM# (YOUR ID#). And can you give me the check number? (RECORD) Great. You can send that to: BAM 30 Lafayette Avenue Brooklyn, New York 11217 ATTN: TELEFUNDRAISING

Thank you for your generous gift, Mr./Ms. _____ .

There's one last thing I wanted to mention to you. If, like many of our friends, you are a subscriber to one or more of our programs, and getting the best possible seats is a priority for you, you may be interested in supporting BAM at the SPONSOR level. As a Sponsor, in addition to enjoying all the benefits already described to you, you also receive PRIORITY handling of your subscriptions through out Patron desk. You also receive a newly released edition of THE MAHABHARATA, the play by Jean-Claude Carriere, and translated by Peter Brook. A gift of $125 would entitle you to all these benefits as a Sponsor of BAM. Can I put you down as a Sponsor, Mr./Ms. _____ ?

Thank you so much for your generous gift, Mr./Ms. _____ . By the way, would you know of any friends or relatives who might also be interested in supporting BAM? (RECORD NAMES AND PHONE NUMBERS)

Thank you again, and have a good evening.

# TELEFUNDRAISING OBJECTION RESPONSES

## I DON'T WANT ANY TICKETS
I'm glad to hear that, Mr./Ms. _____ , because I'm not *selling* tickets! I'm calling about a terrific program we have called the Friends of BAM. (RETURN TO POINT OF INTERRUPTION)

## $75 IS TOO MUCH FOR ME
In that case, Mr./Ms. _____ , you may be interested in supporting BAM at the next level. For a gift of only $45, you still get: 2 passes to each scheduled working rehearsal over the next 12 months, your Friends of BAM newsletter, a 20% discount at the BAMSHOP, and access to our exclusive Friends of BAM telephone line for ticket information. It's really a terrific value, and best of all, you'll be helping us to continue our work in arts education for schoolchildren. How does that sound?

## $45 IS TOO MUCH FOR ME
I can understand that, Mr./Ms. _____ . Actually, a gift of any amount would be doubly appreciated. First, because it would bring us that much closer to our goal, and second, because when we apply for grants, major corporations often look to see not only how much we are able to raise on our own, they also look at how many people have given. In other words, three people giving $25 each means more to us than one person giving $75. With that in mind, Mr./Ms. _____ , is there any amount you'd feel comfortable giving?

## WE'RE TOO FAR FROM BAM
That's fine Mr./Ms. _____ , because...(as I said, I'm not calling about tickets)...this is something you can participate in no matter what part of (New York/the metropolitan area) you live in. (RETURN TO ORIGINAL SCRIPT AT POINT OF INTERRUPTION)

## DON'T GO TO BAM (ANYMORE)
Well, I'm sorry to hear that Mr./Ms. _____ , but even if you don't attend BAM (anymore), our Friends of BAM program is one that you may be interested in. (RETURN TO ORIGINAL SCRIPT AT POINT OF INTERRUPTION)

## ALREADY GIVE TO OTHER CULTURAL INSTITUTIONS
That's great Mr./Ms. _____ . Then I know you appreciate the need for public support for the arts. I've spoken to quite a few people who also support other cultural institutions, and what some of them decide to do is rotate their support from year to year. (RETURN TO ORIGINAL SCRIPT AT POINT OF INTERRUPTION)

## RENEWALS - DIDN'T GET THEIR INVITATIONS LAST YEAR
I'm sorry to hear that Mr./Ms. _____ , but if that's the case, you'll be pleased to hear that we have a new Membership Director. So far, he's organized two open rehearsals this season and both went very smoothly. We're certain you'll find membership services much improved this year, and we'd appreciate the opportunity to win back your support. Can you help us with a gift of ($75/$45/any amount)?

## I PREFER TO GIVE BY CHECK
That's great Mr./Ms. _____ . I'm so happy to hear that you've decided to help us. But, may I ask what your concern is about using your credit cards?

(Courtesy of The Brooklyn Academy of Music)

## NO - YOU MAY NOT ASK WHY!

I understand completely, Mr./Ms. _____ . I wonder, however, if you can do me a favor. Do you have your checkbook nearby? (PAUSE) It would be very helpful to us if you can write in the "notes" section of the check: TM#(your ID#). And can you give me the check number? (RECORD) Great. You can send that to: BAM 30 Lafayette Avenue Brooklyn, New York 11217 ATTN: TELEMARKETING

## FEAR OF FRAUD

Well, Mr./Ms. _____ , you're not alone in feeling that way. Many people I speak with are hesitant to give their credit card numbers over the phone for just the same reason. However, what most people don't realize is that consumer laws protect you from any unauthorized use of your credit card. If you should ever notice a charge on your statement that you are not responsible for, simply deduct that amount from your payment, and enclose a note explaining the deduction. Actually, Mr./Ms. _____ using your card on the phone is no riskier than handing it to a waiter or a gas station attendant. In fact there's less risk over the phone because your signature is not involved. With all this in mind, Mr./Ms. _____ , can we put your gift on your credit card?

## JUST LIKES TO DO BY CHECK

Well, I can understand that, Mr./Ms. _____ . A lot of people I speak with seem to prefer to do it that way. However, once I explain to them that they'll still get a tax receipt if they put their gift on a credit card, they usually change their minds. For BAM, your gift on a credit card benefits us two ways. First, it lets us put your gift to use immediately, and second, a credit card gift costs us much less to process than a check. Mr./Mrs. _____ , either way, we certainly appreciate your support, but may we put this on a credit card?

## NEEDS CANCELED CHECK FOR TAXES

Mr./Mrs. _____ , if you're thinking ahead to your taxes, I should tell you that all gifts, whether given by check or credit card, are confirmed with a receipt. And, what many people don't realize is that the receipt sent out by the recipient is the only valid receipt for tax purposes. As far as the IRS is concerned, a canceled check to BAM could be a ticket purchase! With that in mind, Mr./Mrs. _____ , may I put your gift on a credit card?

## TICKETS ARE TOO EXPENSIVE

I'm surprised to hear that, Mr./Mrs. _____ , because one of the things BAM is known for is our low price policy. For instance, for our current season of the Next Wave Festival, 10 of the 12 events had many tickets priced from $12 to $20. Even our Mahabharata, which at $96 may seem expensive, comes to only $32 an evening, probably the average price for a Broadway ticket. And, unlike Broadway tickets, revenue from BAM tickets is not distributed to investors. Instead, because we are a non-profit organization, the revenue is continuously recycled toward programming and education. It's a fact that ticket prices cover only half of our production costs. That's why we must turn to our audience members for support. Mr./Mrs. _____ , can you help us with a gift of ($75/$45/any amount)?

## DISLIKED PROGRAM - ARTISTIC QUALITY

Obviously, we cannot please everyone with all of our presentations. That is part of the risk we take in presenting such an innovative program. But, this year's Next Wave Festival received a very enthusiastic response from both critics and audiences alike for a majority of our programming. However, I'm sure you'll agree with us that we will always be successful as long as we continue to provide a forum for exciting and imaginative contemporary artists and works.

### DISLIKED PROGRAM - ADMINISTRATIVE

With over one-hundred thousand audience members attending the Next Wave Festival, we realize that there is the chance that our human error may account for a few problems for some of our patrons. But, please be aware that we are taking the steps necessary to prevent any problems from occurring in the future. In fact, the comments you have offered this evening will be passed on to BAM's senior management for immediate action.

### DISLIKED PROGRAM - SEATING

We are aware that there were some sight line problems and made every attempt during the Festival to either switch patrons' seats, or to alter the performance to provide a clear view for all. However, with over one-hundred thousand audience members, it's impossible to give every patron the best seat in the house. That is why its important to join the Friends of BAM. As a member, you'll be among the first to be notified of upcoming BAM events, like the Next Wave Festival.

### CALLBACK OPENING

Good evening, Mr./Mrs. _____ . This is (YOUR FULL NAME) calling from the Brooklyn Academy of Music. We spoke (briefly) on the (DATE OF ORIGINAL CALL) and at that time you requested that I call you back. Just to refresh your memory, I was calling to invite you to join the Friends of BAM. Which membership level have you decided on, the Donor level, or the Friend level?

# SPECIAL EVENT INVITATION PACKAGE—Letter

Dear :

On Monday October 12th, 1987, the Brooklyn Academy of Music will open its 1987-88 Season with the Fifth Annual Opening Night Gala of the NEXT WAVE Festival, the largest contemporary performing arts festival in the world. The evening will also celebrate the inauguration of BAM's newest performance facility, the BAM Majestic Theater with THE MAHABHARATA, conceived and directed by Peter Brook, to be presented in a special one hour extract especially for the Gala.

The Opening Night Gala promises to be the most exciting in the history of the NEXT WAVE. The evening will begin at 7:00 pm with a Ribbon Cutting Ceremony and Champagne Reception at the BAM Majestic Theater, located at 651 Fulton Street. At 8:00 pm, a special one hour extract of THE MAHABHARATA will be performed. Following the performance at 9:30 pm, guests will proceed to the Academy for dinner and dancing.

_____ , Chairman and Chief Executive Officer of _____ Corporation, is serving as Corporate Chairman for the NEXT WAVE Festival. I am serving as the Opening Night Chairman for the Gala evening with _____ participating as Opening Night Executive Vice Chairman. International dignitaries will be in attendance as well as corporate and foundation sponsors and patrons of the NEXT WAVE Festival.

I hope you will join us in celebrating the NEXT WAVE Opening Night. Tickets for the evening are $500 each. Any ticket purchase or contribution of $1500 (two tickets) or more entitles you to membership in the NEXT WAVE Producers Council. The Council provides annual private patronage for the NEXT WAVE Festival and members receive many Patron Priorities for Festival events. The proceeds from this event will help BAM continue its tradition of presenting New York audiences with innovative programs in the theatre arts, both now and in the future.

An invitation and reply card are enclosed for your reservation.

It should be a great evening!

(Courtesy of The Brooklyn Academy of Music)

# SPECIAL EVENT INVITATION PACKAGE—Invitation

# Index

## Compiled by Estella Bradley

## KAREN BROOKS HOPKINS

Ms. Hopkins is executive vice President of the Brooklyn Academy of Music, America's oldest performing arts center, where she has worked since 1979. Among her achievements have been the completion of successful fundraising campaigns for the academy's NEXT WAVE Festival of the Contemporary Performing Arts and the Royal Gala benefit for the Welsh National Opera attended by Her Royal Highness, the Princess of Wales.

Ms. Hopkins was an adjunct professor in the Brooklyn College Graduate Program for Arts Administration for four years. She has also served as fundraising consultant to arts institutions all over the United States, including Opera America, The Boston Children's Museum, The Tampa Bay Arts Council, Fedapt, and many others.

Prior to working at BAM, Ms. Hopkins was Development Director at The New Playwrights Theatre in Washington, DC and Director of Theater at the Jewish Community Center in Rockville, Maryland.

She graduated with honors from the University of Maryland in 1973 and received her Masters of Fine Arts from George Washington University in 1980. She is married to Antonius Hopkins and has one son, Matthew. She and her family reside in Park Slope, Brooklyn, New York.

## CAROLYN STOLPER

Ms. Stolper is vice president for development and public affairs for AFS Intercultural Programs, Inc., a not-for-profit education organization that exchanges students worldwide. Among her achievements at AFS have been the financing of the AFS Teachers Programs and the development of several corporate joint partnerships. Her work in recent years has taken her to over 12 countries. She has frequently served as a consultant to various arts organizations and has written articles on fundraising and the arts.

Prior to joining AFS in 1985, Ms. Stolper headed development departments at Playwrights Horizons and The National Theater of the Deaf and was associate director of the National Corporate Fund for Dance, Inc.

She graduated from the University of Wisconsin at Madison in Art History and Ibero-American Studies and received a two-year graduate fellowship to attend the University of Wisconsin's Center for Arts Administration from which she received her Master's degree in 1978. She lives in New York City.